THE FACE AND MIND OF IRELAND

by

ARLAND USSHER

"This race is at the same time inferior and superior to the rest of humanity. One may say of the Irish that they find themselves in a false situation here below. Placed between memory and hope, the race will never conquer what it desires, and it will never discover what it regrets."—EMILE MONTÉGUT.

LONDON
VICTOR GOLLANCZ LTD
1949

To
CARL AND LUCY

TO HELP THEM TO UNDERSTAND
THE PEOPLE AMONG WHOM THEY
HAVE MADE THEIR HOME

PRINTED IN GREAT BRITAIN BY RICHARD CLAY AND COMPANY, LTD.,
BUNGAY, SUFFOLK.

CONTENTS

FOREWORD

THIS IS A book of highly personal impressions and memories, and not a reference-work for the student. As in my more strictly philosophical writings (*Postscript on Existentialism*, 1946; *The Twilight of the Ideas*, 1948), I have here again attempted to employ the method of what I call "the continually shifting viewpoint"—which may seem bewildering to those who expect the writer to take up a definite controversial position. As applied to my present subject, this method is an easy and natural one for me, as I have never been able to associate myself completely with any Irish or Anglo-Irish group. Though an Irishman by birth and ("in spite of all temptations to belong to other nations") by choice also, I have a good quarter of English blood; though not a Roman- or even an Anglo- Catholic, I have always taken a deep interest in Catholic philosophy and the Catholic life; though a student of Gaelic, I am no revivalist; and though an offspring of the former "Ascendancy", I never felt any sentimental ties to that class when it was in the ascendant. I have defined the essential Irish quality as a combination of mysticism and irony. If I can claim, for my own thought, that particular combination, I owe it to Ireland; but I am aware that I may offend the Irish public by my indulgence in irony as much as I shall probably exasperate English readers by my leanings to mysticism. I would therefore recommend the more unsmiling sort of "Gael" to skip my 1st Part, and the more solid sort of "Anglo-Saxon" not to attempt my 2nd.

ARLAND USSHER.

I. THE RETROSPECT

My school-holidays were passed in a strange and incredible world—in a time when the Irish people (or such of them as I ever met) were called "the natives", and their dwellings "cabins"; when the first sight I beheld on my return from England was always that of a blind patriarch escorted by a lunatic—a half-naked creature who leapt dog-like in the air with excitement at the approach of the locomotive; when the walls of the local school were hung with lists of phrases in "brogue", which the children were to learn so as to avoid ("Bile the kittle and wet the tay", "Tommy thran me in the river and crooshted me wid shtauns"); when even as a small boy I was constantly addressed as "Your Honour", and shop-keepers told you over their counters that you were "as welcome as the flowers in May"; when old crones spat their "fasting-spit" in your face to bring you luck, and fiery old men waved blackthorn sticks at each other, their lips discharging curses in Gaelic (such as for instance "May the devil tear you from the hearse in front of all the funeral"). At that time market-days were occasions of Hogarthian mass-drunkenness, and on Sundays the small towns suffered a wholesale exchange of populations, thanks to the regulation about "bona fide"—disorderly crowds which fought each other on the way home. Witch-doctors cured mares of farcy by whispering diabolical spells in their ears (one of these was "Come out of him, Farcy, you and I will meet in hell"—a curious mixture of primitive animism and medieval theology); and these cures—explain it how you will—generally worked. There was in those days a thing called County Society,

9

more usually known as "the Quality"—families who drove incredible distances in gigs and barouches to drink tea with each other. The males seemed to be every one of them a captain, a major or a colonel; Ireland was a land of colonels as Hungary was a land of counts, and I was secretly a little ashamed that the names of my father and grandfather lacked a military prefix. From the conversation of these people, whenever it strayed from sport or the iniquity of the Asquith government, there emerged a far-from-flattering picture of the "natives". No Irishman, it appeared, could be trusted so much as half a yard; their language, the Erse, contained no word for "gratitude" (I have since heard the same statement made, probably with as little foundation, about Hindustani, Swahili—in fact almost every language in the Empire); they were taught by "their priests" that it was not wrong to lie or steal, and such of them as were members of the Ancient Order of Hibernians (a harmless friendly-society) took an oath that they would murder Protestants whenever they got the chance; more than this, there were those among them who were not above shooting a fox; and at the same time every word and action of an Irishman was somehow inimitably, incredibly, funny. Young as I was, it struck me that the Irish were a patient people, to put up with the things that were said about them.

At other times my grandfather would take me for walks over the estate and the farms of the former tenants—recently promoted to the status of owners—teaching me the hymns of Mrs. Alexander, and explaining to me the intricate system of rights-of-way. If one of these ex-tenants should ever have the hardihood to close a passage against me, my right course, he told me, was to summon all the workmen with appropriate implements to smash the obstruction. One day we passed a mound of stones in the midst of a stinking morass. "There used to be a large family living here," he said reminiscently; "your poor Aunt Henrietta used to hold her nose whenever she passed by the door. They were *savages*." "Well, what became of them?" I asked, intrigued. "There was some delicacy in the family," he said, "and they all died." (I should explain that in Ireland a "delicacy" commonly means a weakness in the chest.)

It was, in short, the world of stage-Irishry; a good-natured world, in spite of everything. The Colonels, perhaps, did not mean *quite* all they said; and they were badly rattled by the terrible threat of "Home Rule". My grandfather was in many ways a kind landlord, in spite of his failure to connect tuberculosis with bad sanitary conditions. But what is played on the stage is unfortunately never the whole of life; and there was during all this time another Ireland, of which the Colonels had not the smallest suspicion. This Ireland had been reared on a book called "Speeches from the Dock" (Emmet declaring to Lord Norbury that if all the blood he had spilled were to be collected in one reservoir His Lordship could swim in it—Norbury replying by calling him "a wild and wicked enthusiast"); on Mitchel's "Jail-Journal"; on a song which was then sung in patriotic assemblies as a sort of national anthem, and began,

> High upon the gallows-tree
> Swung the noble-hearted three,

and on the patriotic songs of the '40s—very stirring stuff, such as "Who fears to speak of '98?" ('98? Bless you, the Colonels had never heard of it), or such as this,

> How did they pass the Union?
> By perjury and fraud,
> By slaves who sold their land for gold
> As Judas sold his God,

> By all the savage acts that yet
>   Have followed England's track—
> The pitch-cap and the bayonet,
>   The gibbet and the rack.

I acquired this literature in the back-lanes, in mean little shops with a name in the ornate Gaelic characters over the door—an arresting sight in those days, when Irish was still widely spoken (at least by old people) but scarcely anyone had ever seen a line of it written. I had by heart a long, long poem by Sheridan Lefanu about Shemus O'Brien, a '98 insurgent; how I thrilled to his speech in answer to the judge's question whether or no he was guilty!

> My Lord, if you asked me if in my life-time
> I thought any treason or did any crime
> That would bring to my cheek, as I stand alone here,
> The hot blush of shame or the coldness of fear,
> Though I stood at the grave to receive my death-blow
> Before God and the world I would answer you "No!"
> But if you ask, as I think it like,
> If in the Rebellion I carried a pike,
> And fought for old Ireland from the first to the close,
> And shed the heart's blood of her bitterest foes,
> Then I answer you "Yes!" and I tell you again,
> Though I stand here to perish, it's my glory that then
> In her cause I was willing my veins should run dry,
> And that now for her sake I am ready to die.

That other Ireland knew all about the Penal Days, when—as a Lord Chief Justice of the time declared—an Irish Roman Catholic had no existence in the eyes of the State, and the Irish were subjected in their own country to a set of laws which we should compare today to the anti-Jewish laws of Hitler; they knew about the Settlement of Cromwell, when the whole population was ordered to betake itself beyond the Shannon or even further, and all personable wenches were picked out and packed off for slavery to the planters in the Barbadoes— when the pious Cromwellians, as they tossed the babies on their spears, observed pleasantly, "Nits turn into lice";

about the great deeds of the exiled Irish on the Continent, the broken native aristocracy—who, according to Irish history-books (though you will not find the fact mentioned in French ones), won the battle of Fontenoy; about the utter strangulation of Irish agriculture and industry in the 18th Century (see Swift, *passim*); about the Famine of 1846–8, when nearly a million of the people died of hunger amidst the exportation of bumper grain-crops, and the dead and dying together were thrown higgledy-piggledy into pits—as many again expiring of disease in the overcrowded emigrant-ships. All this, and much more of the same kind, they knew. These facts were doubtless for the most part really facts (though I am not sure about Fontenoy), if a little coloured-up in the telling; but they were not much known at that time, except by oral tradition, or to students who had gone to look for them. The history taught in most Irish schools was the history of England; Ireland's history was taught only in such little-known establishments as St. Enda's, the school conducted by an unsmiling enthusiast with mesmeric eyes, Patrick Pearse, whose name we shall meet with again in this narrative. To have a smattering of Irish history gave one then much the same thrill that an inquiring youth today feels on learning "the Truth about the Banks". Sometimes I showed the patriotic literature to the Colonels, to "test their reaction". Their reaction was simple and strong. "Why, it's rank disloyalty and treason!" they exclaimed, gasping like fishes.

The *Encyclopædia Britannica* (article on Ireland) expresses the same astonishment as those Colonels of my boyhood, though in more temperate language: "The famine, emigration and the new poor law nearly got rid of starvation, but the people never became frankly loyal."

Yet there is perhaps a point in the remark—and the pained surprise—though it seems an odd way of putting

it. By whatever steps or stages the change had come
about, the fact was that the country had begun to pros-
per. The patriots were looking at life through books, like
the "ingenious gentleman" of La Mancha. The conditions which had driven the gallant Emmet and the brilliant Mitchel into rebellion had altogether passed away.
The Penal Laws were as dead and gone as the Punic Wars.
The awakening conscience of the English (prodded, if you
will, by Irish "agrarian outrages") had given Ireland
close on a half-century of the most benevolent legislation.
The greater part of the land had passed from the Colonels
to the tenants under the various Land Purchase Acts, on
terms which might have made English farmers' mouths
water; and the Colonels were now, for the most part, living in retirement in their tumbledown mansions, devot-
ing themselves to snipe-shooting or painting in water-
colours. The Irish Parliamentary Party, by its size and
unanimity, held the levers of power at Westminster, to
the continual embarrassment of the English legislators.
The patriots' contention that Ireland was over-taxed was
arrived at by taking a fairly long retrospective glance;
this book must avoid statistics, but at the time I write of
there seemed to be grants and subsidies for almost everything, even down to the construction of hen-houses and
the teaching of Irish. It was doubtless true that the
higher Civil Service posts in Ireland were unlikely to be
given to Irishmen if they were, from the British point of
view, sedition-mongers; no government that I have heard
of, except the French government between the two Wars,
has ever allowed the Public Services to be staffed with revolutionists. But there was no grievous oppression—unless you call by that name the fact that Ireland was a part
of the economic structure of Great Britain. This was a
disadvantage to a country with little natural wealth, in so
far as it hindered her development into a modern indus-

trial state—always assuming that it is an advantage for a naturally poor country to go in for uneconomic industries buttressed by tariffs. The Home Rule Bill of Redmond was of little worth to Ireland from this point of view (the point of view, that is to say, of the potential chiefs of industry). It was indeed about as far from independence as the Income Tax of those days (in which the propertied class saw the End of the World) was—shall we say?—from the Communism of Lenin. Only a people which had grown half-listless about the whole question (or, as the patriots put it, were "sunk in their servitude") would have been bothered with such a non-intoxicating beverage. It gave Ireland control of her schools and her prisons—and of precious little else; it did not give her control of finance, taxation or customs. The Liberal Party indeed regarded anything in the shape of a protective tariff with an almost mystical horror.

However, it was written in the Stars, or the Subconscious, or the Dialectic, that Ireland was to become a separate nation; and revolutions are made by rhetoric and not by reason. The patriots said that England was determined to keep the Irish "a race of helots"—language which, appropriate enough to the 18th Century, had little or rather no meaning in the early 20th. But now there was a full-sized "Counter-Revolution" brewing among the Protestants in the North, to resist the passage into law of the dreadful Home Rule. (A poem of the period by Kipling is a sample of how *they* talked, and probably still talk right down to this day:—

> We know the war declared
> 'Gainst every peaceful home;
> We know the fires prepared
> For those who serve not Rome.)

It was treason, if anything was, and a faint foreshadowing of the various Fascist movements which have made an end of Democracy in so many countries since; but you could not imagine a person like Mr. Asquith having a person like the Marquess of Londonderry indicted for conspiracy under the Crimes Act. The Ulster "Loyalists" belonged to the same culture, tradition and *Ideenwelt* as the English Liberals; the socially impossible "Irish members" did not. These were mere pawns in the Parliamentary game, and it may be supposed that the Liberals were not in too great a hurry to see those useful allies depart, who gave them their compact majority in the House of Commons. The Irish Question was like a woman—you could not live "with or without her". Mercifully the Liberal Government were rescued from this excessively delicate and awkward situation by the outbreak of a World War; Home Rule was shelved "for the duration". The Junkers are said to have been impressed with the spectacle of an England torn by faction, and to have concluded that she was in no position to wage a war on the Continent. If it is true—and it may be—they made the same miscalculation as did the Nazis, when they reasoned similarly from the Oxford Union's resolution "under no circumstances to fight for King or Country". The English, as surely everyone ought to know, mean nothing by what they say in the House of Commons or their other debating-clubs; and they certainly were not going to coerce men of their own breed to please Mr. Redmond. One does not blame them overmuch; but it is unfortunate that their habit of fine talk so often misleads more literal-minded foreigners. It may have cost us two World Wars.

However that may be, World War No. 1 arrived, and the English aristocracy exchanged the comic opera of Liberal and Tory politics for the tragedy of Flandersfields and Gallipoli. I am not English, yet I still cannot think of those holocausts without a certain emotion. The

Irish patriots of course, then as now, were uninterested in world-affairs or in "capitalist wars"—for it is strange how non-socialist Irishmen suddenly adopt Marxist language when referring to the two great world-struggles to repel German aggression. All they felt and said was that if the English were really so much concerned about the fate of Small Nations their charity might well begin at home. I thought then, and I think now, that the position of Belgium and Serbia, recently over-run by invaders, was not *quite* the same as that of Ireland, where the conquest had occurred many centuries ago; that, in fact, a German invasion would have been a serious thing for Ireland as well as for England. But no doubt the English recruiting-officers talked a little too much about the Small Nations, especially when addressing Irish audiences. They even placarded Irish walls with posters bearing the words "When Ireland had no schools Belgium gave you hers". True, of course; but it was scarcely very wise or politic to remind the Irish of the Penal Laws.

But meanwhile the insurrectionary Unionist Volunteer Movement in the North had produced the natural counterblast, a Nationalist Volunteer Movement in the South—less well-supplied with funds and quasi-official encouragement, though numerically impressive. But it was significant—the cloud no bigger than a man's hand—that this movement was launched, not by the Irish Parliamentary Party (who dreaded the return to "physical force methods"), but by those underground enthusiasts who had for long been merely biding their time, and to whom "Home Rule" had never been anything but a bitter mockery. These men were in the practical sense (but in that sense only) realists, and not parliamentary hacks—men possessed with one burning idea, which was "*Fiat* the Irish Republic *Pereat Mundum*"—a kind of man which real Englishmen always find it difficult to comprehend. The mass of the Irish people till then had heard almost as little of them as the Colonels had; but they were very soon to hear more.

My own introduction to the dark ways of political intrigue occurred about this time; and as it was grotesque, and also a little sad, I cannot refrain from telling the story, in spite of its irrelevance. At my school in England I regularly had sent to me the various Irish patriotic and separatist journals, including the organ of the new Volunteer Movement—a publication, both as to style and format, of the most lurid description that can well be imagined. The weekly arrival of these strange sheets gave me a certain romantic prestige among my schoolfellows, and it also brought me into sympathetic contact with a Turkish youth called Hussain Azim Bey, a few years older than myself. This boy's parents (whom he never remembered having seen) had both suffered violent deaths, consequent on their fidelity to the Old Moslem Party—recently driven from power by the Young Turks, the "Party of Union and Progress"; but they had first prudently sent their son to England to save him from being murdered along with them. To avenge his parents, and at the same time to compass the overthrow and destruction of the Party of Union and Progress, were the twin ambitions of Hussain's life, on which he brooded ceaselessly and sombrely. Then suddenly the agents of the Old Moslem Party in England offered him a biggish reward—at the time it seemed to me immense—if he would go to Stamboul and assassinate a certain high-placed member of the ministry. They reckoned, no doubt, that owing to his youth and his long absence from the country he would pass unnoticed there. Full of the fire of boyhood, he immediately accepted the foolish, hopeless, job; the village carpenter was ordered to set about the construction of a box with a false bottom. His political friends duly conveyed to him knives, pistols, ammunition. It says much for his singleness of purpose that he did not begin by making a hecatomb of half the school; for he was subject to violent fits of rage, and the other boys treated him as little better than a nigger. However, he somehow kept a cool demeanour, and at the end of term set off on his journey, his arsenal neatly wrapped and hidden away in the secret drawer of the fine new box. I never saw him again. I heard afterwards the local craftsman had done his task so unskilfully that the secret drawer, with all its contents, fell out on Victoria platform, just as he was about to jump on the boat-train for Dover. One may suppose that this catastrophe did not pass unnoticed; at all events he had no sooner set foot on Turkish soil than he was arrested and sent to some frightful fortress on the Black Sea, where I have not the smallest doubt he long ago perished miserably—beheaded, strangled or perhaps impaled. To Azim I owe three things. Firstly, a hazy knowledge of the Turkish alphabet (I taught him Gaelic in exchange); secondly, my first and only experience of friendship in an English school; and third, I am sorry to say, a tendency to regard all revolutionists as fools or bunglers or both—dangerous to themselves and others. Poor Hussain. . . .

But it is time to come back to Erin.

Redmond had said he was going to "bring the Home Rule ship at full speed into harbour", but this dashing nautical operation had somehow gone wrong. The whole nation now was drilling; the country youths, accustomed to sitting on the walls and spitting through the long Summer evenings, found it a wonderful change to traipse up and down and form fours, to the husky commands of some local ex-soldier. For a people that had never had an army of its own, it was naturally a grand and glorious feeling. They had no very clear idea of what they wanted, but they had been told by the leaders that "it was the right of free men to carry arms"—in the South as well as in the North. Fortunately, perhaps, there were not nearly enough arms to go round, and in the country districts the young fellows had to content themselves with wooden dummy rifles—which naturally evoked the mirth of the Colonels. The latter, however, now began to take a distant and lofty interest in the movement, since Redmond—in a last effort to save the Home Rule ship—had pledged the Volunteers for National Defence.

The creators of the movement, on the other hand, knew exactly what they wanted, and they were not in the least concerned with "National Defence". One of them, Sir Roger Casement, was at that moment in Germany. The great majority of the Volunteer corps had officially transferred their allegiance to the uninspiring Redmond; but they, also, felt not the smallest enthusiasm about Defence—excusably, perhaps, since they had only dummy rifles with which to resist the Hun. By degrees this aimless unarmed body broke up, but the smaller body in Dublin had a few real guns, and their plans were laid.

In Easter 1916, as everyone knows, they struck. The date is now a historic one for all Irishmen, and perhaps—in the infinite interconnection of things—an important one for the world; since it is the greatest turning-point in the history of a race of which it may be said—more truly than of the English—that it has "never spoken yet". Having proclaimed the Republic in words that are not without grandeur, they proceeded to occupy the Post Office, the "Mendicity Institute", Boland's Mill, Jacob's Biscuit Factory and various other centres. (The socialist James Connolly thought, rather pathetically, that "a capitalist Government would hesitate to destroy capitalist property"—apparently forgetting that there was a good deal of capitalist property being destroyed in France

and Belgium at that moment.) They held out with great
courage for a week, until finally forced to surrender by
the British artillery. Fortunately, owing to the bad
British marksmanship, the beautiful Classical portico of
the Post Office was almost undamaged; we may be
thankful that it was before the days of aerial bombing. It
was said at the time that the English Tommies, hurriedly
brought in to reinforce the garrison, did not know where
they had arrived, and spoke with apprehension of meet-
ing the "hill-tribes"; but this is probably a story. Fifteen
of the rebel leaders were executed; most of the other
prisoners were released after only a few months' imprison-
ment or internment. (A young professor of mathematics,
who was reputed to have borne "a charmed life" in the
thickest of the fray, and was the last commandant to surrender, escaped execution by a reprieve—perhaps on
account of his youth. His name was Eamonn De Valera.)
When we think of Thiers' monstrous vengeance after the
Paris Commune, or the Bartholomew nights of Nazi Germany—or even of the suppression of the Indian Mutiny—
we cannot fairly accuse the British of great severity or
vindictiveness on this occasion. This of course does not
detract from the heroism of the Fifteen, who scarcely expected anything for themselves personally but defeat and
death. They knew they could hope for no general rising
of the country in sympathy with them, for the concept of
Irish Nationality was moribund, or slumbering; it was
their deliberate intention to call it into being by the sacrifice of their lives. In that intention they may be said to
have succeeded, as few martyrs have succeeded; more than
anyone else they created the Irish nation we know, as
Joan of Arc created the French nation. Since that dramatic
lightning-flash in the Irish sky there have been no more
jokes about "Paddy and his pig". Whether they were
right, who shall say? History used them, as she uses us all.

In 1916 as in 1798 the Rebels had had one chance, and one chance only, of success in their immediate purpose; that chance lay in aid from the enemies of Britain. As is well known, an attempt was made to send help on each occasion—in 1798 by the French, in 1916 by the Germans; but both attempts "fizzled out" lamentably—largely owing to the lack of any real understanding or co-ordination of plans between the Irish and the foreigners. The architects of these schemes—Wolfe Tone and Roger Casement—were exceptional among Irishmen in having something approximate to a European culture. In spite of my respect for Casement and my very great admiration for Tone, I cannot but feel heartily glad that their hare-brained enterprises came to nothing. If the continental allies had succeeded they would have acted towards us, in their turn, as conquerors; if they had failed, we should have been left facing an England in no gentle mood. In either case there would have been a fearful devastation. One may believe, as I on the whole do, that the Irish might have developed more happily and harmoniously under French domination than under British; but the French could scarcely have made a permanent settlement in Ireland. As for a conquest by Germany, I am not one of those who would at any time have desired it. And to say that either of these Powers would have conquered us only to "set us free" is, surely, the merest dreaming.

In any case the vessel and cargo sent by the Germans to Tralee Bay (which found, alas, no watchers-out to welcome it—no population seething with revolt) was hopelessly inadequate; Casement—disgusted with his hosts—followed in a submarine with the intention, not of assisting, but of stopping the Rising, if it were still possible. (He was, of course, hanged for his pains.) France had done better in '98—she sent two large fleets. The English, who learn in school about the Spanish Armada, do not realise how great was their escape when Grouchy—as he was to do once again on the day of Waterloo—waited woodenly for instructions instead of going ahead. One may say, if one wishes to be romantic, that on two occasions was the fate of Europe decided by the indecision of one dunce.

But Tone's French allies might have failed; and I think the German would have certainly failed—mainly because the Republican movement was not general among the people. The extreme separatists, with their tendency to learn Irish and wear kilts, were in my boyhood looked on as harmless lunatics; as I—who was associated with some of them on the language side—know well enough. They were usually called the "Ireeshuns" (as it were, a conflation of "Irish" and "Grecians"). As for a republic, the word suggested to most Irishmen the atheistical excesses of the French Revolution; the French-sponsored republic imagined by Tone would probably have set up the Goddess of Reason in the place of the B.V.M. Patriots are indeed in the habit of deploring the slave-like apathy of the Irish people, the wretched fruit of centuries of oppression. I think the apathy has a deeper cause than mere "slave-mentality". The Irishman is by temperament a religious realist; he knows instinctively what men of most other races have to learn painfully—that there is very little freedom possible to man on earth. This makes Irishmen, in the mass, bad revolutionists; one has only to look down a list of the more famous rebels from Tone to Pearse to see how few of them were of Irish lineage. I think the paradox of Madariaga contains a small grain of truth—that the Irish only combined to achieve independence from England when they had already become English. There is in the Irish (and I hope there always will be) a strain of "Devil-may-care"—of what the French call, with a different nuance, *J'm'enfoûtisme*. The patriot would no doubt reply that Devil-may-careism is itself a symptom of the pathetic irresponsibility of the slave. If that is partly so I think it may be the reason why "slaves"—men used to the hard and necessary conditions of life—are often so much more attractive than the bourgeois, with his smug and purse-proud illusions of "independence". And whatever W. B. Yeats may have said in his aristocratic scorn of the new Ireland, I believe the Irishman can be almost anything, but not a bourgeois. That is perhaps why he is allergic to the urban, bourgeois, thing which is Marxist Communism.

What is really very astonishing about the 1916 Rising is that it seems to have caught the British completely unprepared. The Rebels went to work in the most methodical manner on the morning of Easter Monday, and had a whole day to take up their positions almost without interference. They had chosen the date partly because it was the feast of the Resurrection (an association with the national resurgence never far from the minds of these mystical patriots), but also from the more practical consideration that on that day the Army would certainly be out of town, disporting themselves at the Fairyhouse Races. The British officers—toddling around the paddock, field-glasses in hand—when they were informed of what was afoot treated the news with the most lofty incredulity; a mistake which cost some of them their lives on the same evening. All this is the more remarkable because the whole history of Irish revolutionism till then had been one long pitiful story of betrayals—of generous impulses brought to nothing by the spy and the *agent provocateur*. Shaw's Peter Keegan in *John Bull's Other Island* said that Ireland might as truly be called the Land of Traitors as the Land of Saints. '98 had been less a rebellion than what we should now call a police frame-up, a fiasco deliberately contrived by the British, who wanted

an excuse for passing the Act of Union. Yet on this occasion the authorities would seem only to have awakened
slowly to the fact that the capital was in the hands of
rebels who meant business. Had the Irish grown more
incorruptible, or had Dublin Castle gone to sleep? I
think both explanations are to some extent true, and
the reason lay in the greater prosperity of the country,
and the fact that the relations between the "Conquerors"
and the "Conquered" had become amicable. The same
desperate conditions that produce heroes also produce
traitors; the trade of the spy in his own land is the last re-
sort of needy and broken men. The whole of the Irish
"War of Independence", from 1916 to 1922, had to my
sense a certain atmosphere of *playing*. There were plenty
of ugly incidents of course, and (both during the Black-
and-Tan phase and the "Civil War") a good many guard-
room brutalities, sometimes meriting the name of atrocities; but there were very few of the usual horrors of
Revolution. That is certainly a matter for unspeakable
thankfulness, and for congratulation to all concerned.
But there is also another way of looking at it; when a revolution can be made without horrors it means, I think,
that the need for any revolution at all has disappeared.

The British, having crushed the "disturbance", as they
called it, expected the Irish would forget the painful incident and help them to get on with the War—a War in the
winning of which they held (with some justification) that
Ireland had also an interest. It was that "darkest hour"
in 1917, when the U Boats were taking an increasing toll
(of every four ships that left Britain only one returned),
and the collapse of Russia had set free eighty German
divisions for service in the West, and they were in truly
desperate need of man-power. They had swallowed conscription in increasing doses (always a bitter pill to the
Briton), and they saw no good reason why the Irish, who

could fight so well in Dublin, should not accept a little of the same medicine. But Ireland, from the beginning indifferent to the War for Liberty, was now cynical and defiant. The sacrifice of the Fifteen Men had done its work; their photographs, on a popular series of postcards, adorned every mantelpiece in the country. Redmond, who after all had achieved some tangible gains for Ireland, lost every shred of favour; he died not long after—a rather pathetic Moses in sight of his Canaan, with his Home Rule tablets left as rubble in the political wilderness. "Who Fears to Speak of '98?" was rewritten as "Who Fears to Speak of Easter Week?"—a composition vastly inferior to the old ballad, and reeking with that odour of sanctimoniousness which has since become such a clinging taint of Irish nationalism:—

> Upon their shield a stainless field
> With virtues blazoned bright,
> With temperance and purity,
> With truth and honour dight;
> So now they stand at God's right hand
> Who made their dauntless clay,
> Who taught them and brought them
> The glory of today.

The Rebels, to do them justice, had been something a great deal more than that. Their effect on the popular imagination was due not merely to the list of their virtues, but to the fact that they represented a new type of Irish leader, who was not ashamed—as men like Redmond were—of the language and the folk-culture of Ireland. Ireland may have laughed at their Gaelicism before—now she loved them for it. These men differed, not only from the old type of parliamentarian, but also from the old type of rebel—who was usually a Jacobin like Tone or a Radical like Mitchel. They had read not only the *Speeches from the Dock* of the back-streets, but the heroic romances of Standish O'Grady and the heroic poetry of

Samuel Ferguson—they were steeped in a glorious new-discovered mythology hardly inferior to that of the Greeks. To them the struggle at that moment convulsing the planet probably seemed far less important than the ultimate rout of the Saxon in the Valley of the Black Boar; the consideration that Ireland had a real stake in the Empire meant infinitely less to them than the fact that the Gaelic was passing away by Connemara turf-firesides. Perhaps none of them—except of course Connolly, the Syndicalist—had heard of Marx, and their journal *Nationality* (in 1917) spoke of Rasputin as a martyred saint. They were, in short, utterly unworldly Don Quixotes—in a country where Quixotes can still inspire warm devotion.

At first, indeed, the reaction to the Easter Rising had been one of stupefaction. An Irish Rebellion "in the 20th Century"! (How often people used to say in those days, about any deed of violence or lawlessness, "What, in the 20th Century?") '98 had become mere blood-and-thunder stuff for Temperance Hall theatricals. And how would this affect the price of our cattle in the English market, which was rising in a buoyant curve? The only people who had been enthusiastic were the looters from the Dublin slums, who carried home in triumph pianos and gramophones on trolley-carts through streets a-buzz with bullets. But the executions changed all that. It is true but futile to point out that the British would have gained everything by an amnesty—nations do not behave in that way, especially when they are engaged in a life-and-death struggle elsewhere. It is likewise both true and futile to argue that they should never have lengthened out the agony—letting the cold news fall drop by drop into the nation's consciousness. A modern totalitarian state would have shot not fifteen but (at a moderate guess) fifteen hundred, and not bothered even to inform the relations—supposing that any of these were suffered to remain in freedom. Be that as it may, the whole country was soon writing poems or singing songs about the Men who Died, from W. B. Yeats—who had once lamented that Romantic Ireland was dead and gone, but now uttered the conviction that "A terrible beauty is born"—to the ballad-pedlars in the fairs. (Somewhere about this time was written the undistinguished "Soldier's Song", later to become the official anthem of the new nation—a not very happy choice, one feels, out of Ireland's rich repertory of patriotic songs and ballads.) The many other men (such as the brother of John Redmond, and the attractive T. M. Kettle) who had also quite recently died for Ireland—in the war against Germany— got no press at all. But it is useless to complain about that. For us Irish "patriotism is not enough", there must be glamour with it; and the khaki was singularly unglamorous—as unglamorous as Flanders mud. I remember an anti-recruiting song of the period that ran—

If any Cockney bounder comes
    Around you with his blarney,
And talks of khaki coats and drums,
    The grand life in the Harmy,
Just wink your eye and answer him
    "I've heard that tale before, sir,
From broken-down ex-Army men
    And pauper tramps galore, sir."

If he should say "The rations
    They would make you love your fate so,"
Says you "The concentration-camps
    Are scarcely out-of-date though;
Your blood-red flag in every clime
    Has blazed o'er crime and slaughter,
'Tis fraud and wrong that made it strong
    Here and across the water."

"Young man, young man, your blood is 'ot,
    Don't credit all you hear, lad,
You loyal Hoirish Paddies
    Made the blooming Boers look queer, lad."

> "I love the Boers who held their land
>   Against your Fusiliers, sir,
> They fought for freedom—so will I,
>   I'm in the Volunteers, sir."
>
> "Now just take this 'ere shillin'
>   And your name will shine in story,
> You'll be a bloomin' 'ero,
>   Wot as fought for Hengland's glory."
> "For England's glory what care I?
>   Shall I my land surrender?
> My heart is true to Roisín Dú
>   To cherish and defend her."*

The new revolutionary movement came to be called Sinn Féin—two Irish words meaning "Ourselves", emphasising as you will either manly self-reliance or bigoted self-love; a description as good or as bad as any other nationalistic catchword. The rural population, for whom nationalism till then had meant passing County Council resolutions and sending some local publican to Westminster (unopposed) to "vote with the Party", found itself suddenly in an atmosphere which was decidedly more bracing, though charged with menace. A provisional *de iure* executive was formed to administer and legislate for the Republic which had been proclaimed in Easter Week; it was to govern with the consent and cooperation of the people, ignoring as far as possible the very existence of the foreign and usurpatory *de facto* government of Dublin Castle. Such a "*de jure* government", though no longer representing anyone or pretending to govern anything, and deriving its *jus* from God knows where, continued in being or in name long after the later Treaty and Civil War, and it may still exist for aught I know. But in 1917–21 the experiment was serious and interesting. Such a policy had long been advocated by Arthur Griffith, the most able of the "Irish Ireland" intellectuals, and the

* From *The Irish Volunteer* of September 19th, 1914, over the name "Rory of the Hill".

first to employ the potent words Sinn Féin; he claimed to
have borrowed it from the Hungarian patriot and libera-
tor Deák, though Hungarians, I think, must have changed
a good deal if such a peaceful programme ever succeeded
among them.* It could have been adopted in Ireland
without any insurrection—only, of course, it would not
have been adopted without an insurrection. It could
have proceeded without any of the murder and arson
which were very quickly to follow—only, of course, they
were bound to follow. Those pacifist ideologues who
dream about "non-violent action" would do well to pon-
der what has happened in India to the movement started
by Gandhi—or what happened in Ireland to the movement initiated by Griffith.

(At the same time it must be said that Griffith's language—unlike Gandhi's—always resembled a cataract of
lava, and was little calculated to inspire peaceful proce-
dures; to send representatives to Westminster, he declared, was like appealing against the Devil in the court
of Hell! As Miss Dorothy Macardle puts it in her en-
cyclopedic work *The Irish Republic*: "His [Griffith's] stirring doctrine of national self-respect and self-reliance was
helping to quicken in the rising generation a spirit that no
half-measures of liberty would content.")

I have no wish whatever to carp at my countrymen's
desire for what so many of them evidently felt, with all
their hearts and souls, was Freedom; even though my
own belief in it did not last beyond my schooldays—it was
perhaps checked and cooled by the tragedy of Azim. Nobody today really regrets the abolition of the Union, or
would restore it even if they could—which is a sufficient
proof that it was a psychological anomaly. The best of

* A friend of mine showed Arthur Griffith's book, *The Resurrection
of Hungary*, to a distinguished Hungarian intellectual. After looking
through it, the latter remarked " It's very interesting, but all new
to me!"

reasons after all, for a revolution, as for a divorce, is that people "feel that way"; the material grievances pleaded in the one case are usually as irrelevant, or as unreal, as the "grounds" alleged in the other. The Irish were unhappy in the British connection, even if—as I am inclined to think—their grievances were mainly of the atmospheric or intangible order. If they were tired of the guffaws of the fatuous Colonels, and the continual challenge implied in the remark that "Of course the Irish could never govern themselves", that is perhaps as good an argument as any case built upon statistics. Bad jokes can become more trying even than bad laws.

And yet, possibly, this is not all. If it had not been for the Sinn Féin movement, it is certain that many, many young Irishmen would have been shoved into the shambles of the Western Front; and the rather ignoble England of those later War-years would have watched their removal with a scarcely concealed satisfaction. Ireland, with her population diminished by the famines and emigration of the 19th Century, might have become as depopulated as the Highlands of Scotland; the Ulsterman of the North-East counties might have become *the* Irishman, as the Lowland Scot has become *the* Scotsman (a fate which I sometimes think would overtake us in any case, if the patriots had their way and Partition were to be abolished). What we now call Eire might have become, one half a bog for the Colonels to shoot over with their small dogs, and one half a prairie for a few farmers to raise their herds on, without the need of other help than that of a lurcher and a stick. Then indeed we could have taken "the Harp that Once" down from Tara's wall, and said to Emmet—who wished his epitaph might be written when his country should assume her place among the nations—"Forget it, son."

I thought then, and I am even more sure of it today after witnessing the Hitlerian horror, that the ambitions of Germany had to be resisted—at almost any price. But even in the late War there were intelligent men in France and other countries—not only mere pacifists, or mere Fascists—who thought the price too great. Shall we, perhaps, all think so after another twenty-five years? May we not then be thankful that *one* country was preserved— by some mysterious destiny, or instinct in her people— from the disruption of European civilisation?

Such portentous thoughts, however, were far from everybody's minds in 1916. As the English looked on "the Rising" as an insignificant brawl in Dublin, so the Irish regarded the conflict between the Triple Entente and the Central Powers as a mere local tin-pot fight in Europe, in nowise differing from the recurrent wars in which Britain, by her arrogant pretensions, managed to get herself involved. The national state of mind was succinctly expressed in such ditties as—

> Up De Valera,
> The rebels as well,
> Indipindence for Ireland
> And England to Hell!

America however was now a belligerent, the victory of the Allies seemed only a matter of time, and the patriots began to turn their gaze to the Peace Conference, where Ireland's case would be heard and the Republic receive the seal of international recognition. Such an expectation was perhaps then not so obviously fantastic as it seems in retrospect, for President Wilson's declarations of War-Aims were pitched in a key of lofty abstract idealism worthy of the patriots themselves, and discontented minorities everywhere were being encouraged to look to the Peace Conference as to a sort of Grand Assize for the righting of all wrongs. "Every people should be left free to determine its own polity"; as Clemenceau mockingly remarked, *le bon Dieu* Himself could not have spoken

better. But it would have been interesting to have asked
Wilson if that principle applied to the Philippine Is-
landers, or to the Southern States in the American Civil
War. As we can see now, the chief result of the catchword "self-determination" was to be the disintegration of
Austria-Hungary and the proportionate strengthening of
the German Reich. But Wilson meant well, and it is perhaps all too easy to be wise after the most disastrous series
of events in history.

(Sinn Féin sent her delegates to the Peace Conference
all right, but, alas, they did not succeed in getting inside
the doors. Wilson, when cornered, excused himself rather
sadly: "You have touched on the great metaphysical
tragedy of today. When I gave utterance to those words
I said them without the knowledge that nationalities
existed which are coming to us day after day.")

While, however, the American Polonius was talking
amiably about "free acceptance by the people immediately concerned", the British were going ahead with their
plans for applying conscription to Ireland; and an Irish
Conscription Bill was actually passed in 1918. It was
patently a folly, if not a crime—though what constitutes
a crime in politics and in war is not at all easy to determine. After all, Ireland had been committed to the War
by her spokesman Redmond; it is true that her mood
had since changed—and catastrophically—but how often
have nations the right to alter their minds? Were French-
men who became pro-Germans after the Collapse traitors
to their former allies, or not traitors? These questions are
to my mind insoluble, like the question of whether Ireland would or would not have the "right" to coerce
North-East Ulster.

The British, having made up their minds to conscribe
the Irish, proceeded to act with determination; the
leaders of Sinn Féin, recently liberated, were re-arrested,

B

and large parts of the country were proclaimed "military areas". On the other side, young men all over the country poured into the ranks of the "Irish Republican Army" as it now came to be called—preferring on the whole to die in Ireland than in the trench-holes, if die they must. Whether the Government would have persisted with their Conscription plan, or how they would have set about it, must remain a speculation; for at this time an event occurred which the world had almost ceased to hope for —the War came to an end. The Central Powers, reduced by hunger more than by military defeat, suddenly caved in. The Home Rule Act on the statute-book should now automatically have come into operation; but the Irish were no longer interested in Home Rule. A month after the Armistice, Parliament was dissolved and a new general election held—the notorious "Hang the Kaiser" election of 1919; in nearly all Irish Catholic constituencies Republican members were returned, over half of whom were at that moment the tenants of prison-cells. They had no intention of taking their seats in Westminster at any time; they were elected to govern the Republic, and such of them as were then at large set about it openly and in a workmanlike way. Civil Courts were established, whose authority was generally recognised by all the litigants; land was commandeered from ranchers and leased out for tillage, the rents—fixed by "Land Courts" —being punctiliously handed to the landlords; "Republican Bonds" were issued; consuls and ambassadors were appointed to foreign capitals. The whole machinery of British administration had, in fact, broken down; a new and functioning nation had grown up almost overnight, a thing which would have been beyond the wildest dreams of the Colonels in my boyhood—many of whom, returning from the War, could scarcely believe what they saw through their monocles. It is possible that the British might now have made great concessions to avoid the inevitable clash—though it is also possible that the "Khaki Government" of 1919 might not. But things had gone far beyond discussion. The Irish demanded a Republic, and by a Republic they meant an All-Ireland Republic—the existence of the armed Volunteer Force in the North was ignored. They were determined if necessary to coerce North-East Ulster as England had been determined to coerce Ireland—exactly how, they did not attempt to explain; they pretended to believe that Ulster, left to herself, would not really fight. What is more, the new men spoke a different language from the British—and I do not refer only to the Gaelic. Redmond could argue with Asquith and Balfour, though they no doubt treated him with a certain condescension, like a Labour Member—in spite of his being in fact, by class, a gentleman. But speech was well-nigh impossible between a man like De Valera and men like Lloyd George and Ronald McNeil. All three were "Celts", and De Valera was possibly the least "Celtic" of the three; but they argued from different premisses, they meant differing things by the same words. You could as soon imagine Mr. Bevin talking in a reasonable way with Stalin, or Stalin with Gandhi, or Gandhi with Franco. The modern world was being born—a world in which you can go to lunch in Paris and tea in Rome and dinner in Cairo, but in which men's souls are divided as by the abysses of interstellar space.

I must now enter upon that sombre period of our history in the present century which Irishmen usually refer to, with their customary fatalism, as "the Troubles". In retrospect, and in a true perspective, those Troubles may look almost trivial, but at the time the things which were done seemed neither good nor pleasant. My countrymen must forgive me if I tell here, in summary, what to most of them is painfully familiar either from experience or hearsay, but what is perhaps less well known to many Englishmen.

Ever since the Easter Rising the situation all over the country had, indeed, been "degenerating". The young men of the IRA and other national bodies had no mind to let themselves be arrested and to have their meetings broken up; they consequently set about attacking all the symbols and engines of British authority—in particular, the smaller country police-barracks. The constables—usually quiet and inoffensive fellows who had the misfortune to be supplied with arms by Dublin Castle—were in most cases suffered to evacuate in peace, if they had the sense to go peacefully; but the barracks were burned to the ground, amid great popular enthusiasm. By the Autumn of 1919 there were very few of the Constabulary left in the country districts—districts which were quite excellently run by the new Republican police, when these were not themselves prisoners. To meet this situation, the British government sent across—in addition to the already huge numbers of military—various auxiliary police-bodies, who soon from their variegated equipment were called collectively the Black-and-Tans. These Black-and-Tans were men of the "tough" type, recently demobilised and unfit for peaceful avocations—men such as later in Germany would have found an instant welcome in the Gestapo. Very soon the population became unpleasantly accustomed on every road, to the sight of wired-over motor-lorries rushing at breakneck speed, bristling with rifles which were constantly fired-off—for any provocation or none. If women or children happened to stop the bullets, that was just too bad; the lame and the halt, who could not run, were often fatally wounded. One casualty of my acquaintance was the half-witted son of strongly Unionist parents. Persons who looked suspicious for any reason (as, for instance, by keeping their hands in their pockets) received little "benefit of the doubt". Terror led to more and more frequent ambushes, and to summary executions of the unhappy "constables", whose duty it was to furnish the new police with information. In revenge the Black-and-Tans, and sometimes the military, would "shoot up" the nearest village or small town—the inhabitants making for the cellars, if they had any. Often houses or whole streets were gutted by fire; sometimes peaceful crowds were given a volley of bullets for them to think about. After 10 o'clock—later after 8—the citizenry were confined indoors by a curfew order; then the search-raids would begin. When a house was raided, the door—if not unlocked quickly—was burst or shot open, and every object on the premises that could conceal arms or documents was ripped or smashed to smithereens. Sometimes some member of the household would be taken to the barracks for questioning; sometimes he did not return. Sometimes, when the spirit-cupboard had been found and rifled, the family were made to stand in their "nighties" with their faces to the wall, while the party sat down to make a night of it. And so on and so forth. It is enough to say that life was not sweet under the Black-and-Tans.

My only personal experience of the barrack-room was short and unpleasant but not serious. I was taken off my train by the military after a baggage-search (they had discovered a book of 17th-Century Gaelic poetry in my trunk), marched up to the camp, and cross-examined by two officers. They questioned, abused and threatened for about an hour and a half; and—I am sorry to remember—my replies were foolish and insolent. Finally one of them said to the other "Shall we shoot this murderer or tell him to get out quick?" (They referred indiscriminately to Irishmen as "murderers".) They decided to settle the matter by spinning a coin, which—apparently —fell in my favour. I have no doubt it was only their little joke—which I had perhaps deserved by my pert replies—though they seemed not only serious but extremely irate. If my accent and appearance had not been those of a "Protestant gentleman", or if I had fallen among Black-and-Tans instead of Regulars, it is likely enough that things would have ended unpleasantly for me. I was then permitted to "get out quick"—with what nonchalance I could muster—but I thought that never, never would I cross that barrack-yard alive. "Shot while trying to escape" was the phrase used when prisoners were fired on after being let out—a certain distance. It was sweet to find myself in the village pub among sympathising faces, and to be treated for half-an-hour as a popular hero—an honour which I had done nothing to deserve.

During this time everybody who had an ounce of latent Irish patriotism, or even of chivalry, became furiously anti-British. But perhaps today a cooler judgment is possible.

What I have narrated are, after all, the commonplaces of life under a foreign garrison which is subject to constant attacks by *guerilleros*. But also with a difference; for in Ireland there were no mass executions of prisoners or hostages, no huge concentration-camps, no systematic and piecemeal "pacification". The British theory was that the IRA were a gang of common cut-throats, to be rooted out by methods which are the methods of police everywhere in dealing with bandits. This of course was very unjust to the IRA, but the alternative was to treat Ireland as a province in revolt and to crush her by fire and steel. I do not think that that would have been preferable. The official attitude did not, and probably could not, prevent reprisals on the civil population—these were

connived at and even authorised, on the ground that the
local inhabitants had failed to do their duty of assisting
the authorities; but it did, definitely, set bounds to such
reprisals. It is known that some of the generals were continually begging to be given "a free hand"—indeed it was
the constant complaint of the soldiers that they had been
sent to Ireland with their hands tied, as mere "targets for
murderers". The higher military sincerely loathed those
âmes damnées of the Castle, the Black-and-Tans; nevertheless their own methods would have differed from "Black-
and-Tannery" only as surgery differs from a pint of
castor-oil. But Lloyd George knew what he was doing,
and he steadily refused the powers they demanded.

On the other side, it was scarcely reasonable to expect
that Britain should capitulate immediately to a revolutionary organisation which had sprung up in three years,
and which had been carried to power by a wind of popular favour. The Sinn Féiners were, for long, not open to
the smallest argument; for them it was "the Republic, the
whole Republic, and nothing but the Republic". If, *per
absurdum*, the British had evacuated the country without
firing a shot, there would at once have been civil war between the IRA and the Volunteers of the North—a civil
war in which many Englishmen would have gone to the
help of the descendants of the Settlers, and many Irish-
Americans would have come over to assist their own co-
religionists. As it was, there was perhaps more destruction and loss of life caused by rioting in the North (generally, be it said, initiated by the Orangemen) than by the
"war" over the whole of Ireland. A "free" Ireland would
then have been what Spain was later to be. Again, I do
not think it would have been preferable.

Therefore I must say this. In spite of my personal sympathy with many of the Republicans, some of whom were
most brutally maltreated in jails, I think the only course

open to statesmanship was the one—in the main—which Lloyd George's government actually pursued; namely, to exercise just sufficient force to wear down the Sinn Féiners, until they should be in a mood to consider a workable compromise. It was, if you will, neither altogether decent nor altogether honest; the Archbishop of Canterbury might repeat piously "You do not cast out Beelzebub by Beelzebub"; but in politics the practicable alternatives are sometimes all of them "dirty choices".

Ireland, by her brave endurance over two years, showed that she was indeed in earnest; England, by not hitting too hard, and by giving way at the right moment, did the most that a Great Power can be expected to do. It is the only way in which the game of politics can be played or in which such fateful bargains can be struck. And everything has worked together for Ireland's advantage in the end.

The calumny that the IRA were thieves or murderers is not heard today; as a matter of fact, they were exceptional among guerilla fighters—at least up till the Treaty —in being almost entirely free from the bandit element. Their discipline I can attest from a remarkable personal experience. After the demolition of the RIC barrack in my district, the wife and children of the police-sergeant had been offered by us a refuge in a part of our house, whither they were escorted in safety by the chivalrous incendiaries. Then, after a few days, came an anonymous letter from some ruffian, giving us notice to eject these "frinds of the inimy" or be prepared to take the consequences. I immediately sought out our local member of the republican "Dáil", Cathal Brugha (an Irishism for Burgess), later one of the bitterest of the extremists in the Civil War. Like most members of that legislature, he was then "on the run" and his addresses were known to few, so that to find him was no very easy task. At last, how-

ever, I got the right directions, and he did me the honour
to receive me; having heard my complaint, he at once
promised the appropriate orders would be sent to the
local Volunteer command. From that day, for many
weeks, an armed guard turned up nightly to protect the
wife and children of an RIC sergeant—and ourselves,
who were known to be out of sympathy with their movement. They refused all offers of convivial hospitality;
they took the most serious view of their duties. Naturally
the same men (though personally friendly) would, if com-
manded, have "burned us out"; but, up till the Treaty at
least, there was very little quite senseless burning.

I know of few atrocities committed by the IRA during
this time, and of those few chiefly from rumour. The
most advertised "horror" was the famous Bloody Sunday,
when the Sinn Féiners put fourteen Intelligence Officers
"on the spot". The victims received a pompous funeral
in London, but—given the conditions of guerilla fighting
—it is hard to see what else the Irish could have done;
and General Crozier (in "Ireland for Ever") has shown
the devious paths which these men had been treading. I
have heard it maintained that these murders were doubly
execrable because they happened at night, when the officers were discovered virtuously sleeping; I have also
heard it argued that these executions were doubly called
for because the English brutes were in fact surprised in
scenes of godless revelry. The former view is at least decent; the second seems to me very odd, though I know
nothing of the facts. But both, I think, are rather typically Irish ways of judging.

It must be remembered that the Republicans had not
been ruffianised, as had many of the Black-and-Tans and
even the military, by the experience of four years of real
war. But beyond this—having seen what some other
peoples are capable of—I believe the Irish to be a mild

and gentle race. Their violent passions escape into literature, or at least into a conversation full of literary violences. The more brutal sort of crime hardly exists in
Ireland; the patriots, who denounced Synge's glorious
comedy *The Playboy of the Western World* as a libel on Irish
home-life, entirely missed the point—which was simply
that no parricide had in reality been committed. Whether
or no it was true in the Heroic Age (as legend affirms)
that a lady hanging with jewels could walk unmolested
through any part of the kingdom, it is—I think—true today, and would have been true at the height of "the
Troubles" so far as the Irish were concerned. Rough men
in other lands will pick up lethal weapons when they are
drunk and in a rage—one can scarcely glance at any
French "faits divers" column without reading "Paysan
Assomme sa Grand'mère à Coups de Hache" or the like—
but in Ireland such undesirable acts are extremely rare.
I have seen a man trying to disengage his friend—who
had in fact intervened on his behalf—from a drunken
brawl; as he held his arm he kept repeating "Think of the
poor souls in Purgatory."

I do not think the Irish mildness is due to especial
goodness of heart—there is far more real kindness in Germans, when they are kind—but rather to that introverted
Fear of Life which is the key to so much that is good, and
so much that is not-so-good, in our national character.
But to this I shall return in its proper place.

For all that, the war conducted by the IRA would not
seem to speak in favour of the romantic notion of the
"Celts" who "went forth to battle but always fell". On
the contrary, the Irish gave proof of a dogged and (to
their enemies) most exasperating tenacity. Owing to
shortage of arms there were never more than 3000 at one
time on the "active list". The instance of their patient
stubbornness which made most impression on the world

was the slow death from hunger-strike of Terence Mac-Swiney, Lord Mayor of Cork—an event which received tremendous popular featuring in France, where the idea of a man deliberately refusing *la bonne chère* to the point of death seemed a stupefying novelty. M. Rivoallan (in *Littérature Irlandaise Contemporaine*) explains it to his countrymen as "l'une des traditions les plus irlandaises qui soient, celle qui consiste à se laisser mourir sur le seuil de la personne qui vous a fait du tort"—a derivation which I find unnecessarily far-fetched.

By the Summer of 1921, however, the weight of superior armament and numbers—becoming more and more freed from restraint—was beginning to tell. As the fiery Miss Macardle, the historian of the Republican effort, has to admit, "the shortage of ammunition was taxing the resources of the Volunteers to the utmost. They were re-filling old cartridge-cases, making bombs out of bits of gas-piping, and, in the cities, converting rifle into revolver bullets. Their active force had been greatly reduced by captures." Lloyd George had already cunningly got a "Better Government of Ireland Bill" passed into law, which had no other effect than the desired one of establishing a Parliament in Northern Ireland; "Partition" had become a *fait accompli*. Now he thought the moment was at last ripe to propose a Truce and invite the rebel leaders to a Conference. Naturally the Colonels were scandalised—"shaking hands with Murder", etc.—though it is true that by this time a few of them had become thoughtful and unhappy.

The account of the Negotiations still makes dramatic reading. Lloyd George confronted the Sinn Féiners with all that charm and finesse which none knew so well as he how to employ. A friendly note was at once struck with a comparison of the Welsh and Irish languages; it appeared that Welsh had no word for "republic"—what was the

Irish word? The party scratched their heads. "Pob-lacht" of course, but that was a recent coinage—the older word was "saor-stát" (free state). "And a very good word too" said Lloyd George, smiling meditatively.

The business once fairly under way, President De Valera proceeded to give his famous imitation of a stone-wall. It was excellent as a beginning in bargaining, and may in fact have had the effect of raising Lloyd George's bid. But De Valera had not come there to bargain; the weak had, ludicrously, come to dictate terms to the strong —to say "Take it or leave it".

The deadlock duly reached, the President withdrew from the Negotiations, and left it to his colleagues to loosen it. This again would have been perfectly normal and proper if he had intended them to strike a bargain, but in fact their hands were—theoretically—tied. The chief spokesmen of the new mission were Griffith and Michael Collins—Collins, the Scarlet Pimpernel of the I.R.A., a man of daring *coups* and hairbreadth escapes, a personality who in conference was to impress such an antagonist as Birkenhead, a man whom any less gloomy generation of Irishmen should have adored.

In parenthesis, one wonders whether Irishmen have ever loved *romantic* characters. Did they, for instance, ever really love Wolfe Tone? Yet I have read no chronicle so full of the spirit of youth and adventure as Tone's Diary—a "boy's book" among the dismal annals of revo-lution, though illumined by a man's mind. In his passion for his young bride, his certain premonition of early death, his irrepressible joviality, he reminds me curiously of John Keats of the *Letters*. But to return.

Lloyd George had at once seen in Griffith a man with whom he could talk—a practical economist and not a futile ideologue; possibly also (though this is merely my own conjecture) a man of Welsh stock. He more and more detached him from the party and treated with him alone—or in company only of the intelligent Collins. Griffith had never cared tuppence about the word "Republic"—as already mentioned, the Hungarian liberation of 1867 was his working model—and he had always hated War. It appears that he was technically at fault in coming to terms with Lloyd George without "reporting to Dublin", for the "plenipotentiaries" had—absurdly—not been given plenipotentiary powers. But Griffith was not the man to be stopped by red—or green—tape. He knew what he wanted, he saw the fruit of his long life's labour within his grasp—the fruit which he had grown from a tiny seed while Ireland lay under the black frost of the Parliamentary Party, in the weary years when he was the only "Sinn Féiner". He managed to win Collins to his side—probably because Collins was in a position to know, better than any man, that the I.R.A. was at the end of its tether; and the other delegates, in their turn, protesting they would ne'er consent consented. (Two of them afterwards, rather feebly, tried to run away from their signatures.) It is conceivable (though, to me, very far from obvious) that he could have got even better terms than he did; but his opponent had all the big guns in the Council Chamber—and, more literally, outside it. Then the Treaty was published, and Ireland had a brief hour of joy—until De Valera spoke.

For alas, it is the universal experience of mankind that it is easier to begin a war than to end one. The Volunteers throughout the country, accustomed now to an adventurous William Tell sort of existence on the hills and in the glens—quartering themselves at their "sweet will" on a well-wishing countryside—felt no very powerful urge to return to grubbing in the potato-patch. Moreover—to adduce a more respectable reason—De Valera was the proud and stately type of leader whom Irishmen in their hearts really respect—he was neither "stagey" like Collins nor prosaic like Griffith; and he had around him the aureole of Easter Week. Nevertheless it was not pleasant to see Griffith and Collins (the two foremost of Ireland's champions, one with the pen, the other—so to speak—with the sword) howled down by a rabble of juveniles in my local town. (The same thing happened in every other town in Ireland.) To quote once more the excellent Miss Macardle, "He (Griffith) must have seen himself . . . as a man who, having spent himself in awakening the dormant ardours of nationalism in his people, had aroused passions greater than he could moderate and ambitions higher than he could satisfy." (More shortly, he was, alas, hoist with his own petard.) It was then that was revealed to thoughtful minds the ingratitude of the Mob in all its beauty and plenitude. I have, since that time, seen other mobs at work in other lands, and I know the Thing that I hate, and which all sane men should hate too. "You're lions, aren't you!" shouted Collins, "Dandy-lions!" It was the only part of his remarks that I caught, amid the boos and missiles.

Within the year Griffith and Collins were both dead—Griffith (a man of iron physique) worn out by his "fool-driven land", Collins shot from an ambush (or murdered, as you prefer it). The Republicans scribbled, unpleasantly, on his grave "Push over Mick and make room for Dick". ("Dick" was Richard Mulcahy, Michael Collins' successor as army-chief, and Minister for Education at the time of writing.) To such depths of schoolboy shockerdom the exalted mood of Pearse's Easter Week Proclamation was to fall. (That Proclamation began, "In the name of God and of the dead generations from which she receives her old tradition of nationhood, Ireland, through us, summons her children to her flag, and strikes for her freedom". Fine words, but it is easy to see the danger of self-deception lurking in such incandescent faith.)

I will not waste my readers' time with the wretched wrangles about the form of the Oath of Allegiance ("faithfulness" versus "recognition", etc.), which involved us in a tragi-comic Civil War, and nearly brought about the grave misfortune of a return of the British. They resembled nothing so much as the controversies which enlivened the Councils of the early Church. Like the theologians of the first centuries, Irish public men still combine a primitive combativeness with a Byzantine tortuousness of mind; their politics have something of the character of the Book of Kells. Even Bernard Shaw, who counts himself a realist, wrote his longest work around the fantasy that a Bushman's baby should—and could—receive the same income as Henry Ford.

But the parallel of the Early Christian Fathers reminds one that metaphysical distinctions generally have a meaning, at least to the persons who make them, and sometimes a very important meaning for mankind at large. Certainly to an Englishman—and indeed to anyone with the smallest sense of what are called "realities"—the arguments about the Oath to the King were maddeningly futile. But the Irish, almost alone among peoples, have never lost intuition of a different plane of reality—the plane of those non-rational feelings which ultimately motivate all action. The difference between the British and the Irish meanings of "loyalty" goes to the roots; I will return to it later. It is enough to point out here that the English Monarchy has very different "overtones" for an Irishman from those which it has for an Englishman. The King of England is not merely a secular prince—he is the head of the English Church, he sits in the seat of Henry VIII and Elizabeth, he pledged himself on his accession until very recently to persecute papists. (The first British monarch to omit the formula was George V—a lapse at which George Moore affected great indignation!) More than all this, the peculiar aura of sentiment—almost of reverence—with which the English invest royalty is to an Irishman something very alien; he reacts to it as an Orangeman reacts to "popish idolatry". It touches some irrational metaphysical nerve in him, and however much he may believe in the Empire on reasonable grounds—however respectful he may feel in general towards the reigning House—he suddenly becomes a furious rebel. Once this is grasped it is not hard to understand how Irishmen could make a civil war over the Oath to the King—even some of those (I admit there were few) whose minds could stretch to perceiving the benefits of a Commonwealth.

In this respect—as in one other—the Irishman is something of a puritan, and he really should stop abusing Oliver Cromwell. Catholic or Protestant, he never really cares a hang for ritual; he has nothing of the English love for pomps, forms and ceremonies—nor, unfortunately, of the Latin European's capacity for taking them lightly and filling them with colour. They simply irritate him, and he wants to cry out "Take away that bauble!" It is the same slightly austere temperament which makes our country-people really prefer the bare whitewashed wall to the roses round the door and the honeysuckle peeping in the window.

But these rather discursive considerations do not alter the fact that the "Civil War" was a sorry farce. One leader boasted that the number of men in arms against the Free State in Dublin alone was greater than the total throughout the country against the British had been; he might have added that a surprisingly large proportion of them were generals! That things were approaching comedy must have been realised by the people at large, to judge by the jokes that were current at the time. The Republicans chalked up on a wall the stirring words "Anastasia O'Ryan confined in Maryborough Jail"; another hand scribbled underneath it the comment "Birth of a Nation". Someone christened the Republican Party "the Women and Childers Party". (The reference was to the diminutive T. E. Lawrence, Erskine Childers, who played a large and destructive part in the whole of the Irish "War"—the most enigmatic of those many Britons who have seemed to be the friends of any country rather than Britain.) Indeed an alarming feature of that time was the Monstrous Regiment of Joan of Arcs; the women's auxiliary organisation, Cumann na mBan, were die-hards nearly to the last woman—one oratrix declared that "all the plain women of Ireland were for the Republic". I had occasion to call upon the wife of one of the Republican leaders; my reception was very different from that accorded me by the polite and efficient Cathal Brugha. I was treated for half-an-hour to a tirade about the blood of martyrs, and I scarcely got out of her house without being handed a white feather.

But the Civil War had also its tragic side, which should not be under-estimated. A Black-and-Tan, stepping onto the boat at Kingstown, is said to have shouted to the crowd "So long, I'll soon be back again to separate you!" It nearly came to that; but in fact Tan was eclipsed by Super-Tan. There was much less than there had been of anything that can, by any stretch of language, be called fighting; but there was more blind destruction, more brutality behind barrack-walls. The leaders could not but know that they had no faintest chance of success, and that the war they waged could only complete the ruin of their already sorely tried country; nor had they the excuse of the Easter Week rebels that they were arousing a torpid nation. The Civil War left a cloud of bitterness

and cynicism which infected all intelligent Irishmen o
my generation, as if such a country and such a people
were not worth dying for or living for. "Kathleen ní
Houlihan", said one of my friends—a distinguished Gaelic
scholar—"has turned out to be nothing but an old sow."
The Republican *enragés*—who disobeyed their Church
and were often denied the sacraments—gravitated in
many cases to anti-God bolshevism, and a perversity like
that of the Nazi in the Second World War who said "We
are killing in order to recover our belief in life." Such a
perversity will always have its poets, and there is much of
this feeling in the later poetry of W. B. Yeats—himself a
supporter of the Free State. In the end this aimless blood-
lust seemed to communicate itself to the government
side; seventy-seven of the Republican leaders were executed—a total compared with which General Maxwell's
fifteen in Easter Week seems a mere *hors d'œuvres*—but
this time the weary population did not put the heroes'
photographs on post-cards. One of the first of the victims
was Erskine Childers; his death appears to have been almost over-zealously pressed for by a no less enigmatical
character, the ambitious and calculating Kevin O'Higgins, who was himself to die by an assassin's bullet in
1927. O'Higgins the student of Macchiavelli, who might
have been the Irish Mussolini, Ireland's most able public
figure (as some think) during the century—had he perhaps read, in the eyes of the Englishman, a sombre purpose kindred to his own?

I never met Childers, and I do not profess to understand what motives could have driven so brilliant a personality upon such a dingy tragedy. I have called him an
Englishman because his whole mental and moral forma-
tion were English, though I am not unaware that he had
some Irish blood. I confess to a certain—perhaps un-
generous—feeling of resentment towards him for the

harm he did us, which I do not feel against those whom Louis McNeice calls "Ireland's ignorant dead"; for he should have known better. However, all who knew him testify to his having been a fearless and an honourable man. So were all the Republican leaders—all honourable men; at least there was no trace of petty self-seeking in them. The noblest Roman of them all was Eamonn De Valera, with his face of a saint by Ribera; and I do not intend it merely as a sneer. Ireland has been fortunate—I now think—in having in him a Lincoln who survived the Civil War which he brought about. In spite of some policies of his which have seemed to me to touch the very acme of foolishness, he has never once lost his dignity of speech and bearing. Griffith and Collins were wiser than he in 1922—who can doubt it?—but he outclasses both of them, I think, by his general tone and temper. He has set his face against persecution and mean victimisation—an example which should make some Orange leaders bow those "stiff necks" of theirs with shame; he has affirmed his faith in democracy when it would have been easy enough to have grasped at dictatorship. He is —in the best sense of that discredited word—a liberal, and yet has always preserved a certain aristocratic aloofness; he has walked with the great ones of the earth at Geneva, but still has never lost touch with his verities. He is, in spite of all, of the line of Grattan and Parnell and Swift— the Uncrowned Kings of Ireland. It is therefore with regret that I have had to glance at his responsibility (second though it perhaps was to that of Childers) in the Great Folly of 1922.

Having handed the squealing Free State baby into the keeping of Collins and Griffith, the British proceeded to scurry out of the greater part of the country with tremendous relief—in most cases not troubling to ascertain whether the forces who took over from them were "Pro-

Treaty" or (as they generally were) "Anti-Treaty". It was perhaps well that they did so, for otherwise the Pre-Truce conditions would speedily have re-established themselves. But the effect was that Ireland, South of the Border, suffered a six months' interregnum, when there was no functioning government and (in most country-districts) no law—for the I.R.A. were too much at sixes and sevens to give very great heed any longer to the "guardianship of the peace". Yet there was little more of ordinary crime than in other years—that is to say (though it is true there has been some degeneration of late) practically none at all. This has always seemed to me a most amazing fact—difficult even to imagine in most other countries —which should in fairness be remembered beside the senseless political violence which was then raging, or beginning to rage. That the Colonels did not all have their throats cut was entirely due to the innate decency and forbearance of the Irish people—those "natives" whom they had for so long spoken of as knaves and scoundrels. It is the more remarkable when one considers that the Northern Protestants were indulging, at that very moment, in a pogrom of Catholics falling not far short of East European standards of ferocity. The Colonels were entirely without means of defence, having given up even their shot-guns in deference to British Army orders which only they obeyed; yet no one even tried to take their watches from them. It is, alas, true that very many of their ancestral mansions were sent up in flames. But this was in pursuance of the drastic and ruthless plans of the Republican leaders, and dictated by some imagined "military necessity"; it was not a popular outbreak. The owners were afterwards compensated, and even over-compensated, by the Irish Government—so far as the destruction of historic homes and glories of 18th-Century architecture can be compensated for at all. But the incendiaries seldom came to steal. They obeyed their mysterious "orders"—often with very sincere expressions of regret.

However, if the Republicans felt that the Treaty was a surrender and a personal betrayal, I can assure them that the Colonels felt so no less; for they also, after their fashion, had an emotional attachment to the land of their birth. Strange and shocking as it must sound to Irish nationalist ears, they had actually looked upon Ireland— its mountains, rivers and noble Georgian towns—as *their* dear country, which their ancestors had won for the Empire with their blood as they had won Canada from the Redskins and Australia from the Blackfellows—had transformed from a miserable chaos of warring tribes into the orderly colony of a great and progressive nation. A slight difference of point of view, you see—and, like most points of view, theirs had something to be said for it. They or their fathers had built the cities, they had laid out much of the magnificent landscape, disinterestedly they had mapped and surveyed, explored and burrowed. Now they and their homes were left unprotected to the tender mercies of gunmen, who boasted openly and impudently that they had "cleared the British out". Standing where we stand today, I am entirely in agreement with those gallant gentlemen in holding the British Commonwealth to be the last great bulwark of decency and civilised order, as I feel equally at one with Irish patriots in regarding Eire as the last stronghold—almost—of the Christian European culture and tradition. Perhaps the world's single faint hope lies in a harmony and understanding appreciation between the two; that is the belief which has made me lay aside philosophical *belles lettres* to write this book. Ireland is the soil where two great traditions meet. I think it is time for them not only to meet but to exchange bows.

But in 1922 the Colonels almost faltered in their allegiance to the Motherland—I have heard them cry out in their agony that they would never again tread her soil—just as many of the Republicans had really ceased to care what happened to Ireland; for both were nourishing deeply wounded feelings. The one extreme might have turned altogether towards some sort of anarchic Fascism, the other towards Communism, if such ideas had had meaning or able exponents in the Ireland of the time; fortunately they had not, and the great moment passed—possibly not to return—for these two nightbirds of 20th-Century nihilism to alight on Holy Ireland. There was to be another moment—during the height of the "Economic War" in 1933, Europe's black year; but then the spirit was not the same—the "devil" had died in the Irish people. De Valera's party had become more or less responsible governors, and the sons of the Colonels—those who remained—had become good Irishmen. The latter now live on the best of terms with their Catholic fellow-citizens and form—I think, if it is not my prejudice—a very valuable element in the State. They are even beginning to drop the slightly snobbish-sounding description of themselves as "Anglo-Irish". The better-read among them are proud, as they should be, of men of their own stock like Tone and Lord Edward Fitzgerald, Charlemont and Grattan—who were the first Irishmen to think in terms of an Irish nation; and they realise something of what the 18th Century meant by an Irish gentleman.

At the time of which I write, we—in common with all our "county neighbours"—were awaiting nightly a visit from the gentlemen of the petrol-can and the match-box. And here I should like to relate a conversation which, though strictly irrelevant, is not unamusing, and which—as the saying is—"could only have happened in Ireland". My mother, wishing to preserve from the flames a collection of Chinese bric-à-brac (some of that "loot from Pekin during the Boxer Rising" which has furnished so many English and Irish country-houses), sought out, by dint of infinite inquiry, a musty and unvisited museum in our county-town. Having discovered the porter—himself seemingly as old and forgotten as any exhibit in the place —she asked him for the addresses of some of the museum-committee members, to whom she could hand over her curios. He replied by four laconic and terrible sentences, delivered in a tone of withering resignation worthy of a Stoic philosopher: "They are all dead. They have all gone to another world. It may be a better one. *It cannot possibly be a worse.*" Often and often in later years I have thought of that strange old man—a steward of the deposits of Time, and guardian, as I see him, of its Secret.

Six months without law! Yes, I too have lived in Arcadia. But I have a feeling that, if the situation had lasted twelve months instead of six, we should have seen a most encouraging growth of "class-consciousness". For there were very ominous moments. A farm-strike was organised in my own county, which soon took the character of a veritable blockade of farmers by the "workers". Farmhouses were surrounded by cordons of pickets in relays, who halted everyone on entering and intercepted supplies —even produce of the blockaded farms. Cows, of course, had to be milked; so the strikers milked them—and sold, or themselves drank, the milk. We, the besieged, lived— not happily—for two months on tinned sardines, and other foodstuffs which could be imported by devices known to smugglers; for the pickets were chivalrous and did not press their investigations too far, especially in the case of ladies. Sometimes friends on motor-bicycles would "run" the blockade with parcels. In the evenings our bewildered proletariat, more than half full of drink, would gather in dark swarms on the roads, fatuously waving red flags, and listening to tirades from little black-coated rascals. A sensational news-sheet, printed somewhere in Dublin, was handed round among the demonstrators, in which our funny little strike was represented as a sort of Western Front of the great World-Revolution, which was causing Privilege in all lands to tremble and clasp its ermine tighter. My neighbourhood had in fact held out longer against the menaces of the strikers than the surrounding areas, and one week I read the following alarming announcement:—

DUKE- AND BARON-RIDDEN AREA NOW BEING SLAMMED.

. . . Here therefore is the keystone of the employers' edifice. It should, of course, have been hewn away first, and it would have been if the men had been ready, with a resultant collapse of the whole edifice, but the rest of the structure has now been battered down, and the foundations will speedily be rooted out.

It was a publication rich in song, and a poem that I remember entitled "the Slave-driver" deserves to be recorded—an interesting example of the excessive Irish addiction to alliteration—

Punish the slave-driver, bell him, exhibit him,
Show him around for a while ere you gibbet him,
Pitchcap and thumbscrew and maul him and mangle him,
Torture him, tar him, and finally strangle him;
Dig a deep hole in the dirtiest clay for him,
And hang the impostor would ask you to pray for him.
Creature of greed and apostle of evil,
Scorned of God and esteemed by the Devil.

(The last two lines of the stanza seem a little tame after such a stirring beginning. But we were in Ireland still, where these contradictions are commonplaces.) The fact that decent workmen—many of them life-long friends of their "masters"—suddenly began to read such pretty verses with gusto, might enlighten some of our chicken-brained intellectuals as to the reality behind the phrases they repeat ("class-war", "liquidation of the property-owning classes", etc.). But this was only the overture—the "piece", happily, was not played; for contrary to most people's expectation, the Treaty party was at last able to push the futile patriots out of the way and begin to govern.

During the ten years which followed the events I have related, Ireland was governed by the most capable and disinterested group of young statesmen who ever—I should think—midwived the birth of a nation. That is indeed a standing reply to the taunt of the Unionists that "of course the Irish could never govern themselves". The devastation of the foolish Civil War was quickly repaired, confidence was restored, budgets were balanced—in the face of strikes, sabotage and sectional whimpering of every sort; capital was attracted to a country in which—it had been the fashion to repeat—"nobody but a fool would invest his money". The three plagues of almost every new state during the '20s—inflation, expropriation, persecution of minorities—were avoided. The murk of the provincial towns was dispelled by the Shannon Electricity Scheme, Dublin—proverbially dirty—was French-cleaned, home-grown beet-sugar began to make its appearance on our tables. Schemes for the licensing of bulls and the grading of eggs and butter—which in many districts savoured of heathenism, and which the British would never have dared to introduce—were rigorously enforced. City corporations, whose corruption had become a joke for the Abbey stage, were suspended and replaced by efficient commissioners. Lastly, by their part in the discussions of the Imperial Conference, the Free State ministers assisted notably in the transformation of the Empire into a free Commonwealth—a work which few people in Ireland know, or wish to know, anything about, but which may yet prove to be the most important political development of modern times.

For all this, the ministers of the Cosgrave party received precious little thanks, and indeed went about their beneficent labours, during all these years, in peril of their lives. Like the German Weimar Republic, the Free State was regarded by the populace as a hateful foreign imposition, and its legislators—like the often admirable statesmen of pre-Hitler Germany—as liveried servants of the Enemy. They were returned to power, in successive elections, simply because there was no alternative but a relapse into chaos. Those Republicans who were elected refused to take their seats, so that they were a total loss to their constituencies—even though, while ignoring the parliament of renegades in Dublin, they continued to appoint their own Ministers of Fisheries, Foreign Affairs, Fine Arts, etc. The only effective reminders which these people gave of their existence were the murders and other outrages that they from time to time committed. These misdeeds were usually condemned by the leaders, but without great severity, and always with emphasis on the moral that such things might be expected to continue happening in a Free State, though not in a Republic.

And now, even as I write, I am conscious of an aftertaste of weariness, an enormous boredom with the unrealities of Irish politics which assailed us Bright Young Things in the '20s. To think that in the strength of youth our heads should have been caught in a cloud of bugaboos—like the gibbering ghosts of the Greco-Roman eschatology—a swarm of empty phrases about the Felons of our Land, the Dead Generations, Cromwell's Massacre of Drogheda, Sally Kavanagh's Untenanted Grave, the Oath, the Governor-General, the Blood of Martyrs, etc., etc.—and all this in a century which, whatever its evil, is

passionately devoted to realism—oh, many a drink was
called for to drown the thought of such impertinence. We
seemed to ourselves like the unfortunate persons in the
fairy-tales who were granted three wishes, to their un-
doing; with the first, Ireland had gained the Black-and-
Tans, with the second the "Irregulars"—now many of us
would have spent our third wish in putting back everything as it used to be. A friend of mine, a *farceur* who pretended to take himself seriously, even tried to start an
agitation to induce the British to re-annex the country
and run it as a Crown-Colony. (The same ingenious
young man had a scheme for a new religion of Mutual
Confession—an anticipation, with a difference, of Oxford
Groups—by means of which various notorious public
characters should be assembled in one room, made to tell
their crimes, and afterwards blackmailed severally.) It
was how we felt, and of course we were wrong and over-
impatient—unjust, also, to the men who were rebuilding
amid the ruins. We ignored their prosaic but necessary
work, and concentrated our indignation on their Acts for
prohibiting divorce and for prohibiting the sale of "evil
literature"—measures which might have been expected
from any Irish Catholic government, and which, con-
sidering the social atmosphere of Ireland, did little more
than register prohibitions that would in any case have
been effective, in fact if not in form.

As already recorded, for many years after the petering-
out of the Civil War, the party of Mr. De Valera continued the farce of standing for a parliament in which (on
account of that unhappy Oath) they had no intention of
sitting—a sort of strike of legislators which made democracy ridiculous. At length in 1927 the Cosgrave government sought to stop this nuisance by passing an Electoral
Amendment Act—intending candidates should either
take the Oath at once or else spare themselves the trouble

of presenting themselves for election. In this dilemma Mr. De Valera's party hit upon an ingenious procedure—which was simply to take the Oath, declaring beforehand they regarded it as an "empty formula", and then, so soon as they should become in turn the Government, to pass an Act abolishing it (which in due course was done). Charming—and so simple! And if somebody had only thought of it sooner, how many brave men need never have faced firing-squads in the cold dawn—how many historic monuments might still be delighting the anti-quarian—how many innocent persons, blown to smither-eens by road-mines or flogged to flitters in barrack-rooms, might have been spared all hurt! "By such slow degrees" as has been said "do the most useful and seemingly the most obvious arts make their way among mankind"—and at the cost of what suffering!

In forcing the Republicans to come into the Dáil, the Cosgrave government had shown disinterested states-manship, for now their own fall could not be long de-layed—it took place, indeed, four years later. (I avoid the meaningless and, to a foreigner, unpronounceable party-labels Fianna Fáil and Fine Gaedheal—the "Heroes of Destiny" and the "Tribe of Gaels".) The accession to power of Mr. De Valera seemed at first to undo with one stroke all the good work of the previous ten years, and to empty the Seven Vials of the Apocalypse on the Irish nation; but at this date we may concede that he gained as much for his people by a tremendous gamble as did Mr. Cosgrave and his henchmen by their sound conserva-tive methods. Moreover it was well that he came to power when he did. The activities of the more extreme Republicans—who never accepted the *petit arrangement* about the Oath—had forced the Cosgrave government into passing a series of "Public Safety Acts", progressively increasing in severity, of which the third in 1931 practically abrogated the Constitution. Had they remained in office, it seems probable that they would have been driven—by the logic of the situation, as well as by certain ideological trends in their own party—into some form of Fascism. The light-hearted '20s were passing into the grim and murderous '30s, and the wind was beginning to blow from Nuremberg; Ireland, in her turn, was to have "Blueshirts". De Valera at least was no Fascist, and he has never thought in class—or sectional—terms; during the Abyssinian war and the Spanish Civil War he kept a course very distasteful to many of his Catholic country-men. He has been able to draw the teeth of the Diehard Republicans with the help of a whiff of patriotic oratory, where Cosgrave would have had to extract them from a screaming and resisting patient. Finally—however much we may quarrel with some of his methods—we should be grateful to a leader who gave his attention, during the decade preceding the Second World War, to the problem of national self-sufficiency.

As may be supposed, Mr. De Valera's Short Way with the Oath was not much to the liking of the British, who have never been able to understand why the Irish (or for that matter the French, or any other nation) should not pay some sort of homage to their Throne; but they did not make it a *casus belli*. When, however, he proceeded to withhold the Land Annuities—payable by ex-tenants on the loans good-naturedly subscribed to turn them into owners—their patience became exhausted; they retali-ated promptly by clapping very stiff duties on all Irish farm-produce.

The Irish case, as the ordinary farmers saw it, for the refusal of these payments was simply the argument of Communism—from which however they would have been very indignant if anyone had drawn Communistic conclusions; the old landlords, it was held, had been

nothing but plunderers and extortioners who squandered
the sweat of the toilers, as a popular recitation of my
youth phrased it,

> In the cards and the dice and the race-course, and even in
> deeper disgrace
> Which no tongue can relate without bringing a blush to an
> honest man's face.

What right had they ever had to compensation? It might
have been asked in return, by what title then did the present occupiers lay claim to their land, who had been
tenants from these same landlords? for only in few cases
were they the descendants of the original owners of the
soil.   It must be admitted however that the question was
not quite so simple, on either side, by the time the lawyers
had finished with it; their "findings" ran into many
volumes, and Mr. De Valera had the support of some
eminent British jurists. Also the fact that Britain was at
that moment in difficulties over her debt to the U.S.A.
put her in rather a false position in this controversy. Mr.
De Valera indeed (on the old principle that England's
embarrassment is Ireland's opportunity) thought the
occasion good to claim a huge sum for alleged over-
taxation by England during the last century, and a
further—unspecified—sum for injury sustained by Ireland through Britain's departure from the Gold Standard!

The immediate effect of the penal duties was the dire
impoverishment of the farmers, most of whom had voted
for Mr. De Valera's policy. Their condition was palli-
ated, to some very slight extent, by "bounties" or sales-
discounts to the home-consumer—a fashionable idea
among credit-reformers, but which at this time produced
an orgy of black-marketing in coupons. There was a
comic and brutal incident when a government-fixed sum
promised for calf-skins produced a rush of farmers to

slaughter and skin their calves—often with blunt or inappropriate implements—a massacre which nearly had
the effect of extinguishing the cattle-trade outright.
Equally incredible scenes (recalling, with an added
horror, Lady Gregory's farce *The Jackdaw*) followed on a
guaranteed price being offered for old cows to be made
into meat-meal.   It is not to be supposed, however, that
the rash policy of the Government was much blamed; for
—as Macchiavelli might well have remarked—there is no
surer way in which a Prince can endear himself to his
subjects than by involving them in some misfortune, in
repelling which he may seem to be standing courageously
in the breach. The farmers, moreover, were allowed to
keep half of their annuities for themselves, if they were
still lucky enough to make any profits—though the other
half (contrary to their first exuberant expectations) had
now to be paid to Dublin; and Irishmen are wont to
think more of a penny made by devious methods than of
a shilling earned in the ordinary way of commerce. On
the whole, the majority continued to regard the default
as a very sound idea, as well as being extremely patriotic.

It was then that, being—like so many others—hard-hit
by the dispute (from which I did not benefit by so much
as half an annuity), I made my first and last application
for a public post, in sending the following letter to the
press. (It was not printed, and my application was never
considered.)

SIR, Since I am informed that there is a demand for
a man (or woman) of Irish birth to fill the office of
hangman (or -woman) to the Irish Free State, I beg to
state that I shall be ready at any time to take up work
in this capacity, as there appear to be no other open-
ings for young men of good family and liberal views in
the Twenty-Six Counties. As I understand that the

clothes, no longer required by the executed subject, form part of the perquisites of the office, this should incidentally solve—in a fashion—not the least of the problems confronting the father of a family since the launching of our Government's "economic war". I beg to add that my piece-work rate for the execution of political malefactors would be lower than for persons driven to crime by economic need, as the work would be naturally less irksome (and the clothes of better quality). I may mention that as a translator of Gaelic poetry I should hope to pass the bilingual test, necessary for all appointments in the Free State, and doubtless essential for taking down the last remarks of prisoners, which are made, presumably, in Irish only. It will no doubt be a deep satisfaction to those homicides who have tasted public office and dignity to know that they are being hanged by a gentleman—a satisfaction which will be entirely mutual.

Yours etc.
ARLAND USSHER.

The last sentence, I freely admit, was in bad taste. But it was a time when tempers were high.

The wisdom of Mr. De Valera's Economic War may be questioned, but there can be little question that his ideal of a—largely—self-supporting Ireland was the right one. In a world which hurtles more and more insanely between boom and slump, trade-boycott and war, the philosophic counsel to "cultivate the garden" has become the clearest economic sense. Ireland's dependence on rearing cattle for the English market was the one really unhealthy feature under the Union—a perversion which had nothing on earth to do with "oppression", and which was generally lost sight of amid all the patriotic vapourings. It was no village fanatic, but the great Bishop Berkeley, who queried (and that at a time when the population was double what it is today) "Whether, if there were a wall of brass a thousand cubits high round this kingdom, our natives might not nevertheless live cleanly and comfortably, till the land, and reap the fruits of it?" It has been the way of living of the Irish to export their own excellent meat, wool, eggs and fish in return for inferior qualities of the same commodities, and often for the unsold part of their own export. That is still to a large extent the situation today, though De Valera has done more, perhaps, than any man in waking us up to its unnaturalness; the poorer classes, I am informed, acquired the habit of eating Irish meat during the Economic War, and have not since relinquished it. The country of one industry is apt to find itself, by some sudden shift in world-demand, a country of no industry; even if the Economic War seemed well-calculated to bring about that very calamity, it at least taught us a lesson which we may hope will be not soon forgotten. It looked indeed like scuttling the ship before a raft had been provided, but it might be argued that the shock was needed to set us Irishmen thinking about raft-construction. It is probable that the fullest possibilities of economic nationalism cannot be realised without national, or regional, currencies; but such questions are too technical to be dealt with here. Mr. De Valera's industrial programme is open to criticism in detail; it has produced much sheltered inefficiency, and some corruption; but at least he has steadily kept before him the aim of a balanced economy. A foundation has been laid to the work of making Ireland a nation in the only practical sense of that word—the sense of a home for men rather than a breeding-ground for emigrants and bullocks.

The Economic War continued to engross political passion in Ireland, while the shadow of Hitler grew longer

c

and longer over Europe. The Fascist leaders had a would-be emulator in the fatuous police-chief General O'Duffy; his "Blueshirts"—at first created to secure legitimate free speech for the Cosgrave party at elections— became for a time the hope of Big Business-men and disgruntled ex-Unionists. They adopted the language of continental Fascism, not omitting the baseness of anti-Semitism, and denounced Mr. De Valera (probably untruly—if the point has any importance) as being of Jewish origin. (It is significant of the deplorable change that had come in the world that it had occurred to no one to make this suggestion—true or false—during the Civil War.) The story of how the General was brought to see W. B. Yeats, and obliged to listen while the poet discoursed to him on Hegelian immanentism and Gentilean neo-idealism, is of a high order of comedy—a fit subject for a Max Beerbohm cartoon. Yeats' later Fascist tendencies were certainly regrettable, and he in fact favoured O'Duffy with a Marching-Song for the Blueshirts—which however was little likely ever to become a popular "hit". But it is a sign that the Irish political climate was still healthy that the gang-leader came to call upon the poet; in many countries at this time the poets were paying their respects to the bravoes.

(General O'Duffy, having failed to set the Liffey on fire, eventually formed an Irish brigade from among the more adventurous of his followers, and went to the aid of Franco. It was afterwards said—whether truly or not I cannot tell—that his legion had the rather unusual good fortune of returning home in greater force than it set out.)

The end of the trade dispute came in 1938, when De Valera personally negotiated a settlement with Neville Chamberlain. The latter agreed to waive all outstanding claims in return for the payment of a lump sum, and moreover—fateful decision—to relinquish those naval ports the use of which Britain had reserved under the Treaty. This latter concession was in accord with the much-decried Appeasement Policy of the Chamberlain government, and (like the whole of that policy) was strongly criticised by Winston Churchill; Irishmen at least should abstain from the Leftist denunciations of the "Municheers". Mr. De Valera's settlement was an achievement almost equal in historical importance to the Treaty of 1921, but it had also an ironical resemblance to it in the aftermath which it produced. For just as the British surrender of '21 had unleashed the violences of Mr. De Valera's Republicans, so the surrender of '38 led to an outbreak by those Diehards who regarded De Valera, as he himself had regarded Griffith, as no better than a traitor, and who were shocked—as he on that earlier occasion had professed to be—by the continuance of "Partition". Did he, one wonders, experience anything of that eerie sense of "history repeating itself"? The new campaign took the very unpleasant form of the laying of bombs in post-offices in Britain, by which a number of inoffensive persons—innocent, most likely, of the smallest knowledge of Irish political matters—were blinded or otherwise injured. This is the last chapter (to date) of the rather tedious tale of Irish revolutionary violence; for in the midst of these excesses the Second World War arrived, giving us somewhat weightier preoccupations.

The manner in which Mr. De Valera steered his country through the tempests of the next seven years is an achievement which compels admiration, whatever may have been one's attitude to the vexatious question of Neutrality. The matter has been so little understood in England that a word or two must here be said about it; broadly, I think the Irish were justified in their neutrality, though not in their indifference. The anger felt by so many English people was due simply to the unfamiliarity of the idea that Ireland is a separate nation; once this premiss is granted, the neutrality of Ireland seems no more shocking than that of Sweden or Portugal. The Englishman's concept of nationality is, on the whole, racial; he has always—except in war-time—regarded the German as a sort of Englishman, and the Irishman as a more primitive variety of Welshman or Scotsman. It was no doubt extremely irritating to the English that Ireland should benefit by the protection of the British fleet, while giving no assistance in return; and it was easy to forget that the Irish contributed largely—though unofficially and rather in a "Soldier of Fortune" spirit—to the British armed forces. But the Germans could have obliterated the few Irish cities in a single night's bombing-raid, and plunged the island back into the anarchy from which it had so lately emerged. Small nations may have less to lose absolutely than Great Powers, but they have very much more to lose relatively, by the ravages of war.

It must be confessed however that the complete apathy of my countrymen, as the Panzer-divisions steam-rolled liberty out of one country after another, was more than a little exasperating to anyone who felt himself to be, not only an Irishman, but also a European. To listen to them one might gather that by holding aloof from the fray they were not only exercising a right but upholding a principle—the great and sacred principle of Neutrality! Apart from the majority who took no manner of interest in the War—or at most the detached and comfortable interest which one might take in a serial "thriller"—the views of most educated Irishmen during these years might be summarised somewhat as follows. England, they would tell you, was a "liberal" or secularised state, Germany was a "pagan" state—and there was no great difference between them; a socialist state, like Russia, combined of course the viciousness of both. Ireland's place, if anywhere, was with a possible "Latin block" of Italy, Spain and Vichy France, which—with the diplomatic aid of the Vatican—might exert a mediating influence between Germany and Britain. The defeat of France was above all a shattering blow to the power of the Grand Orient—the wicked and godless engine of continental freemasonry. Hitler himself was a "bad Catholic"—that is to say, a lax one, but not lost to the faith. The persecution of the Jews, though of course carried too far, was a part of the movement in all Christian countries to throw off the domination of cosmopolitan finance. Broadly speaking, the difference between England and Germany was that between a satiated wolf and a starved one. Hitler was a patriot, he had saved Germany, etc.

In all these views there was a fraction of truth (except, of course, in the absurd misconception of Hitler's character and religious attitude), but, like the opinions of Irishmen on so many subjects, they were those of seminarists. The picture they combined to give of the European fact was somehow out of proportion; it was an attempt to force the complex, changing and terrifying reality into abstract and bookish categories—for the besetting sin of the Irish, of which the former mathematics-teacher De Valera is the perfect example, is not passion but pedantry. The Irish had never pictured or tried to picture—shall we say?—the Warsaw Rising, when more than a hundred thousand of the citizens were taken and butchered, after a blow for freedom more desperate and heroic than Easter Week. They had never pictured or tried to picture the extermination-camps of Poland, and the horrible sealed wagons crawling eastward from every European city. They had never pictured or tried to picture the nights of terror in which millions of families were waiting, year in year out, for the torture-boys of the S.S., their hearts leaping at every noise in the street. They had never seen—and perhaps only he who has seen *can* picture—the utterly unparalleled bestiality that was Nazism. If you had spoken of any of these things to an Irishman at that time, he would most likely have retorted on you with Amritsar and Bachelor's Walk and Kevin Barry's broken-hearted mother. Ireland, that has missed every great historical experience, has missed this one also, and perhaps we may be thankful—the dreadful 20th-Century experience of the Abyss.

Well, it may be replied, *que voulez-vous?* Nations do not fight unless their own interests are directly attacked—and rightly and properly so. To preach the duty of crusades is to turn every local war into a universal war, and make of every nation every other nation's keeper. If this were honestly admitted there would be less cynicism in politics —cynicism which is always the brother of sentimentalism. Certainly the English who looked on, in the frozen immobility of the "phoney war", at the obliteration of Poland—the Americans who waited for the insult of Pearl Harbour to precipitate them into the struggle—the French who . . . but I refrain!—certainly these nations have no right to sit in judgment over the Irish.

Be all this as it may, Mr. De Valera's achievement in keeping his country out of the whirlpool was a consummate piece of statecraft, which Irishmen will always remember with legitimate gratitude. He might perhaps have put the final touches to his masterpiece by coming into the conflict in its later stages, as a not unprofitable "gesture" (cynical though it sounds in blunt terms, this would be a natural enough piece of political sagacity in a small and weak nation); but such suppleness is certainly not in his nature, and Ireland would never, I think, range herself—even as a matter of diplomatic form—with Soviet Russia. As it was, his policy may yet prove to have given a final *rationale* to his whole dubious and tortuous career. But for the quarrel with Britain which De Valera kept so exasperatingly alive, he might never have got the return of the Ports in 1938; if Ireland had not had the Ports she would assuredly not have been able to preserve her neutrality; if she had not preserved her neutrality she might now be in the grip of the same terror and chaos that tortures so much of the civilised world today.

At present Ireland benefits by Britain's wise tolerance of anomalies; Eire's international status is undefined.* From the point of view of the English, and of the rest of the world, she is a British Dominion; but she regards herself as a "Republic in External Association with . . .", and loses no opportunity to act in conformity with that view of the matter. Fortunately the British have no mind to go to war over a word, as many Irishmen saw fit to do in the '20s; and the Treaty of '21 was in fact drafted with such deliberate vagueness that a quasi-Republican interpretation of it could even then have been sustained. But Eire's ministers and envoys abroad, and their foreign *vis-à-vis* in Dublin, are accredited (respectively) by and to His Britannic Majesty; and circulation—or even migration—between Britain and Eire is almost unhampered by restrictions. There is possibly in this situation something more than Gilbertian comedy; it may well be that Irish pedantry and English empiricism have in this case added up to real inspiration. If, in days to come, any of the Dominions should wish to detach themselves from the Commonwealth—or if (which is not impossible) other nations should show a disposition to attach themselves to it—Mr. De Valera, with his formula of "external association", may be found to have given the needed solution. It would be an ironical achievement for the most tena-

* This paragraph was written prior to the recent revision of Anglo-Irish relations.

cious of Britain's foes—the strange man who twice nearly ruined his country sooner than call her a "Dominion", but who (I verily believe) nourishes no hatred of England in his heart.

In all this narrative I have tried, as far as possible, to avoid moral judgments; for the current of national destinies cannot be banked within moral laws. All action, but especially political action, belongs largely to the irrational part of our life, and if men were entirely reasonable there would be no history. Certainly, by any rational standard of social conduct, there should never have been a bullet fired in Ireland from 1916 downward —not even if we take the rule of the Catholic Church, which wisely recognises no excuse but "intolerable oppression" for rebellion against the constituted authority. And the method of warfare employed by the rebels— that of ambuscade and assassination—was scarcely very glorious, though no doubt it was the only one possible. None of the rebel leaders, certainly, deserves any haloes; Griffith was a ranter and Collins a gunman, De Valera is a narrow political doctrinaire, Pearse was a really shocking sentimentalist who called hatred of England a "holy" emotion, and who turned mere schoolchildren into snipers. But what of it all? These leaders had enough of nobleness in their natures to make them an inspiration for ordinary men, and between them they created a nation which may have a new word to give to the other nations. Before 1916, Ireland was regarded as a mad country in a civilised world; today she may be considered a relatively healthy and hopeful country in an increasingly mad world, a state—marvel to relate in the nineteen-forties—free from social, racial or ideological strife. Her fate might have been very different were it not for the men who died in Easter Week. Perhaps that is their best justification.

II. THE ASPECT

Whenever i happen to visit English friends I am assailed with a number of questions which—owing to certain difficulties connected with terms and definitions— I find it exceedingly difficult to answer. I mean such questions as: Are the Irish as priest-ridden as ever? Why do the Irish—lovers of liberty—put up with a Censorship of Books? Why are the Irish so unforgiving? Will the Irish ever become loyal? Now that the Irish are "free peasant-proprietors" should not all be well? What has become of the Irish sense of humour? etc. My fellow-countrymen, when interrogated in this fashion, usually reply whatever comes easiest to them, while laughing up their sleeves at the simplicity of their English hosts. But this book is written, primarily, to explain the Irish to the English, and I must make the attempt to clear up these obscure matters. The questions are fair questions, their difficulty only arising from the fact (which I hope I may be excused for repeating) that the Irish are a separate nation, and that words have not quite the same meanings on the opposite sides of the Channel.

Irish Protestant readers, if any have done me the honour to read so far, may have felt slightly aggrieved that, in speaking of "the Irishman" simply, I have usually had in mind the Catholic Irishman. Catholic Nationalist readers may have been equally—though less understandably—indignant at my identifying "the Irish Nation" with the Twenty-Six Counties, the area known prior to Mr. De Valera's reconstruction of 1937 as the Free State and ever since as Eire. For it is a part of the official creed that the worst of Ireland's grievances against Britain—that of the dismemberment of the *corpus*—still shrieks to heaven for redress. To such objectors I would reply that since the people of North-East Ulster have seen fit to exclude themselves from the new Ireland, and so far have shown not the slightest disposition to revise their attitude, it seems both unreasonable and impertinent to consider them as a part of the nation. The Boundary is certainly a grave disadvantage to almost everybody concerned, and is necessitated largely by the Penny Dreadful religious delusions of the Orangemen ("Maria Monk" etc.); but as these delusions show no sign of weakening, it must be considered more or less as one of those unwelcome innovations which have "come to stay". During the late War I frequently made the suggestion—which was however somewhat coldly received—that since many Irishmen declare themselves ready to die to abolish the Boundary, the Irish Government might propose a reasonable bargain: that we would make common cause with the United Nations, but only on the condition that we could declare war as, ourselves, a united nation—an independent and undivided Republic. The Ulstermen no doubt would have angrily refused to discuss the proposal, but they would thereby have put themselves in the wrong with the British and still more with the Americans, and have incurred all the odium for our abstention. However as my countrymen never thought of making this fine diplomatic gesture—as no Irish government would have had the people with it in making it—I cannot, since then, take very seriously their heat over the subject of the Boundary. Mr. De Valera, to be sure, always gave "Partition" as the main reason for our remaining out of the War; but since he did not and could not add that upon the removal of "Partition" we would come into it, his argument was not at all impressive.

(At the same time it should be pointed out that a united *neutral* Eire would possibly have tipped the scales against the English in the Battle of Britain, and would have been too tempting a morsel for the Germans to leave unswallowed. On this occasion, at least, Eire ought to have been thankful indeed for the Orangemen.)

But there is a special reason why, in speaking of the Irishman, I refer more particularly to the Catholic. It would be hardly too much to say that for an Irish Catholic his nationality is inseparable from his religion— so much so that an Irish Protestant never quite knows to what country he belongs. But for their religion (I do not speak of the policy of the Church, which has usually been loyalist) Irishmen would probably have forgotten Political separatism, as the Scots have forgotten Jacobitism; Scotsmen today, after all, do not trot out Cumberland the Butcher every time that Nazi atrocities are mentioned, as many Irishmen throw Cromwell at you! The Republic of Eire includes, indeed, Protestants of most denominations—not forgetting (rather especially in the farming community) a very widespread and very honourable sect known as "Cooneyites" or "Dippers", a body more resembling old-style Quakers than any modern Nonconformists. But the non-Catholic feels himself far more cut off from his nation than does, let us say, a Roman Catholic in present-day England; he feels rather as a heretical Jew might feel in an Orthodox Jewish community. The life of his countrymen is an intricate pattern of fasts and festivals, pilgrimages and retreats, in which he has no part. He enjoys almost perfect toleration—a toleration, indeed, which ultramontane Catholic theorists like Belloc would regard as nauseously "liberal". There is no public post—from the Presidency downward—from which he is debarred, or for which he cannot compete on almost equal terms with the majority.

But he finds it hard to converse freely or intimately with Catholics, he cannot easily (since the *Ne Temere* decree of 1908) marry or give his children in marriage with them, he tends not to visit at their houses—not so much that he would be unwelcome in them as that he would feel embarrassed by a different outlook and habit of life.   This means that in a nation of under three millions he must seek for friends and intimates, wives or husbands, among a minority of less than two hundred thousand—a minority itself sharply split up by divisions of class and sect.   In these circumstances it would be surprising if the non-Catholic did not feel himself something of a stranger and a "foreign body" in Eire; if he is sensitive, he will sometimes feel even the toleration he enjoys as more exasperating than persecution would be.   It was in such a mood that the "apostate" George Moore said of his cousin Edward Martyn, "Martyn is the most selfish man alive. He thinks that I am damned and he doesn't care!"

For myself, I am always conscious of a displeasure with our young Communist intellectuals, because I know they would probably destine me for the concentration camp—though nothing would please me better than to discuss Marxian Dialectic with them.   How much more then must I feel an undercurrent of resentment against my Catholic acquaintances, who can calmly contemplate me spending an eternity in Hell—though I am interested as much as they, and more than most, in the philosophy of Thomas Aquinas.   I am aware of course that, according to the Church, pious Protestants do not necessarily go to Hell—though they must be content to take the opposite direction with a rather large handicap.   But unbelievers —if they have had the ill-luck to be baptised, at an age when they were unable to protest—almost certainly do; and Spinoza, Schopenhauer or even William Blake would be classed as "unbelievers".   Recently, in my

notes for a radio-talk,* I made the seemingly harmless remark "I am a member of no church". I was advised to
alter this confession to the even more anodyne statement
"I am a non-Catholic". In Ireland, to assert publicly "I
am a member of no church" would be like saying "I am
an unconscionable scoundrel".

And yet, in spite of all, I consider that the Irish people
deserve high commendation for holding to the ancient
faith, in a world that has grown shoddy-minded, which
thinks in press-captions and party-slogans, and has given
itself rabidly to the shallowest of all heresies—the great
modern heresy of mechanised Progress.

For the Irish, almost alone among the nations today,
religion is still the central reality of life, concerning which
discussion is unnecessary, if not dangerous. In England,
as in most other countries, a man's religion is an opinion,
when it is not a mere habit; one may be on familiar terms
with him for years without knowing or caring to inquire
his religion—or, if the subject interests him, it may be a
matter for frequent and friendly discussion. But for an
Irishman—and I speak of educated, intelligent Irishmen
—religion is not really in the field of discussion; and,
since his opinions on all other subjects are conditioned
by his religion, there is really nothing the least funda-
mental which one can discuss with him at all. He is not
"bigoted" in the unpleasant sense of that word—it is
simply that one cannot probe deeply into his mind
without striking against a hard shell of dogma. He is of
the same cast as Hilaire Belloc, who once said with his
usual hearty frankness, "I have no opinions—I have only
convictions". This makes, of course, for a certain lack of
freedom and flexibility in the Irish mental environment.
I do not know if there are debating-societies in Irish
Catholic schools and colleges, but if there are I cannot

* See Appendix.

imagine what the Irish youth finds to debate. In other words, the Irish, for good and ill, are not a modern people—or perhaps it would be truer to say that they have not been through the 19th Century, and hardly even through the whole era of humanism. It is certainly a factor for good as well as for ill. The world is quite plainly returning to a sense of the importance of Dogmas —that is to say, of the intuitive presuppositions of all thinking—and if that movement is not to bring us a night of barbarism, mankind must be willing again to learn by the lamps of the civilised religions. As W. B. Yeats impatiently wrote, "Opinions are accursed", and again, "How but in custom and in ceremony are innocence and beauty born?" In Ireland the question is not so much what a person *thinks* as what he *is*. The distinction has almost been lost sight of in most countries today, where the Self has come to be identified with the mental consciousness—the complex of opinions. In an Irish crowd there are fewer differences of opinion than in an English crowd, but there are many more differences of character —there is far less Old School Tie or New School Tie. Irish people—more especially Irish intellectuals—always strike foreigners as extraordinarily malicious. There is certainly an element of sheerly destructive and dwarf-like mischievousness in the Irish mind; but the malice is at least partly due to the fact that Irishmen are more interested in Persons than in Things.

English people are inclined to assume that the Irish are "priest-ridden" because it is hard for them to imagine a civilised race, at the present day, that sincerely believes in religious dogma. For the English mind is the most un-dogmatic, the most anti-metaphysical, in the world; the Englishman's test of a belief is always "Will it make me a better, healthier, happier human being?" If one reads such a book as Aldous Huxley's *Perennial Philosophy*, one

notices that the author is scarcely interested in the pro-
found differences between Eastern and Western religious
thought; one might almost say that he is concerned only
with the effects of religious exercises upon the functioning
of the glands. The Englishman distrusts all hard-and-
fast definitions—he has an instinct that they "don't work
in real life". Even Cardinal Newman conceived of religious truth as an evolving thing; even your Anglo-
Catholic would seem to be interested chiefly in points of
ecclesiastical history and precedent. But the Irishman's
instinct (and it is the old unchanging metaphysical instinct of all men) is that religion has very little to do with
"real life" or "what works"—that is to say, "real life" is
not, so to speak, really real. Doubtless the Irishman's religion is often—in the modern jargon—"escapism"; but
the very word implies a modern way of thinking. For the
religious man it is practical effort and ambition which is
the "escape"—even though it be a normal and healthy
one.

I once heard a Catholic and a Protestant business-man
arguing about the fact—much vaunted by Protestants
in my youth—of the prosperity and progressiveness of
Protestant countries as compared with the decay and
stagnation of Catholic ones. The Catholic said "You see,
we put our religion before our business"; the Protestant
answered promptly "And we put our religion neither
before nor behind our business but *into* it". The reply was
neat, but one felt they were hardly arguing about the
same thing—by "religion" the Protestant meant simply
ethics, or perhaps that quasi-mystical quality which
business-men speak of (in hushed voices) as "vision".
Today this whole controversy, which inspired Macaulay
to such eloquence, seems very remote; the present world
is not divided between religion and business, but between
those who would retain the possessive pronoun and those

who would not retain it. That is what has come of leaving out the metaphysical note in life and ethics. The very virtues which created the great Protestant capitalism —freethought, self-help and individual initiative—are the most threatened today by the logical development of that capitalism.

It is none the less true however that religion weighs rather heavily in the atmosphere of Ireland. It has been my fate to pass the larger part of my life in a valley about fifteen miles in extent, containing three small and squalid towns; it could boast no fewer than eight convents and monasteries. In such a vale of sanctity one would have expected to find some evidences of uncommon spirituality among the lay-folk. I cannot say that I found many. Their lives were, on the whole, the same sordid round as those of peasants and hucksters everywhere. Their only amusement, apart from over-reaching each other and setting each other drunk, was the very reasonable one of dancing; and this was generally opposed by the parish priests with almost fanatical determination, though without notable success. Some of these priests were, it is true, very impressive and dignified types—in spite of their Jansenistic hostility to every manifestation of the joy of life. But in general the population seemed to get re- markably little return, even of a spiritual nature, on their prodigious investment of devotion.

When the English speak of a "priest-ridden" people they usually have a picture in their minds of a scheming, probably dissolute, priesthood battening on the grovelling superstitions of an ignorant laity. That is certainly very far from the Irish reality. The Irish priests are men of the strictest life and the most unquestioning faith, and they are deferred to—though by no means always obeyed—by the educated as much as by the uneducated. As evidence of the imperfect obedience, I believe that

Mr. De Valera—beloved by the nation at large—has at no time been the first favourite of the Church; and, as everyone knows, the war waged by the Republicans in 1922 was condemned as "mortal sin". Nevertheless it is true that priests bulk very large in the Irish scene; it is the first thing in Ireland that strikes visitors from any other country. What is the reason for this? It seems to me that the question has never been fairly examined.

There are many Irishmen now living whose grand-fathers could remember the end of the struggle for "Catholic Emancipation". It is true that the mass of the Penal Laws had lapsed even before the passing of the Act of Union; but their effects lasted long in poverty and illiteracy, and in a land-system which the most fervent conservative would today scarcely defend. The ugliness of most Irish Catholic chapels, cathedrals and schools is simply due to the fact that few of them were, or could be, built earlier than the 19th Century; yet one constantly hears visitors to Ireland commenting sourly on the poor-ness of "Catholic taste". Thus in Ireland—and in Ire-land alone, perhaps, of Catholic nations—the priesthood have continuously been united in sentiment with the people rather than with the gentry or the Government; in their clergy the Irish have had that rare thing, a popular aristocracy or élite of learning, a class to speak for them and suffer with them. And—as Charles Lever (always a fine observer) accurately foresaw*—the moral and financial insolvency of the gentry, together with the pious nationalism of O'Connell, could have no result but to turn that popular élite into a real and effective ruling caste. This accounts, I think, not only for the prestige of the priest, but for two fine qualities in the Irish *plebs*: a natural respect for learning and letters, and a certain deep and smouldering pride—unlike the poor in

* See *The Martins of Cro' Martin*, Vol. I, Chap. XVIII.

most other lands, they have never, even in their deepest abjection, felt completely abandoned. The ferocious chastity of Irish lower-class women (a subject to which I must return) is in part, I believe, an expression of this pride. Many of the popular songs of Ireland are about Village Lucretias who preferred death to dishonour:

> And when to die a death of flame that noble maid they bore,
> She only smiled—O'Driscoll's child—she thought of Baltimore!

In my boyhood, attracted by the mystery of "the Black Man", I was a frequent visitor at the houses of some of the older parish priests. I found there an atmosphere in which I was completely at home. The bare distempered rooms, which no desecrating woman's hand had cluttered with ornament; the dusty oil-paintings of foreign church dignitaries in stiff robes, with their slow enigmatic smiles; the shelf of Latin books, covered often in leather or parchment, on the strange remote science of theology—crowning a cupboard from which the invariable two bottles were produced, port for ladies and "total abstainers", whisky for good Christians; the conversation, cynical yet kindly, of my host: all this I found in the highest degree appealing and fascinating. So much was I, at such moments, under the spell of this old Roman world that I might have been an easy convert; but so far from any design being practised on my religion, the subject was deliberately made difficult of approach.

One of these *éminences grises* I particularly remember, who might have been the original of Paul Vincent Carroll's creation in his fine play *Shadow and Substance*; a man of deep learning and real culture, he yet strongly reprehended the establishment of a local public library. "Teaching the latest ideas of blackguardism" he called it—though he had, in fact, virtual powers of veto over the books. The only piece of theology I remember from him was the trenchant remark, "If a man does not believe in another world, you may be sure he has some good reason for not wanting to believe in it." Had I been a bright youth in their own communion, I can well imagine that I would have viewed these haters of modernity with different eyes; and in fact the priests of today, who advance in ever new black battalions from Maynooth, seem to me of an inferior stamp—anaemic and petulant rather than shrewd and tough. But, after all, there are few things that have not undergone deterioration in this calamitous century.

So much for the priest in Ireland, and the reasons why he still commands the loyalty and affection of the common man—instead of being nicknamed, as in France, a *ratichon* or, as in Germany, a *Pfaffe*. The Irish priesthood have no doubt their limitations, which it would ill befit me, as a Protestant, to dwell upon with too much insistence; it is perhaps true that they today "have things a bit too easy". In countries which have known no Penal Laws—where the people have no sentimental memories of proscribed priests celebrating Mass on the hillside, with the snow lying around and the drunken soldiery hallooing on the trail, ready to apply the torture of the pitchcap—the clergy have to bestir themselves a little more; they must be a bit more aware of social conditions, and of movements in thought and art which, if not wholly acceptable from a Catholic standpoint, are yet not altogether nefarious and damnable. And among such movements I include even that Communism which at present represents a real threat to our civilisation. From the point of view of almost all Irish ecclesiastics, I fancy, Marxian Communism is an infinitely greater evil than was the National Socialism of Hitler. To anyone however with a live sense of spiritual values, Communism is an assertion —no doubt in a very distorted, materialistic form—of the

Christian idea of human fraternity, while Nazism was an almost wholly pagan ebullition, with a quite horrifying streak of sheer orgiastic diabolism. Most Irishmen would prefer a Christian to a Communistic state, but Christianity will have to show that it has an alternative; the time is past, for good and for ill, when Christians were content to be born and die and obey their betters. "Good works" in Ireland have a Protestant and proselytish sound, having been brought into disrepute by the "Soupers"—well-meaning ladies who went to the starving during the Famine with a bowl of soup in one hand and the Protestant Bible in the other. Catholics moreover have a distrust—with which I sympathise—of the layman or -woman who aspires to "do good"; and Irishmen are quicker to gather round a personality than to "cooperate" for a good cause. Here then is a proper province for the clergy; at present, beyond unfavourably viewing "sin", they would seem (at least as an outsider, perhaps very wrongly, sees it) to concern themselves little with the life of the people. The pamphlets of Mr. Arnold Marsh (to take an example of an Irish economist with a Christian, though not definitely Catholic, outlook) have aroused but slight interest in Ireland. Yet he has shown many ways—some of them perhaps debatable, but all thought-provoking—in which Ireland could be made to flourish like the shamrock, without any Communism.

In the matter of the arts the situation is similar. The latest movements in painting have been all in the direction of order, stylisation and bold simplification; their most promising possibilities would seem to lie in the fields of mural painting and stained glass. Here again is an opportunity for the Church, which is not being grasped.*

* I should not, however, omit to mention the striking work of Evie Hone, which has received a certain amount of ecclesiastical patronage.

Heaven knows I do not ask for the walls of our churches to be covered with the geometrical litter of the Paris School; but Irish artists, with any encouragement, could utilise this often empty formalism to create a new and native religious idiom. Ireland should have her Rouault, her Manessier. In literature the *mésentente cordiale* is still worse—here there is almost open war between the Church and the "intellectuals". The intellectuals, of course, are often foolish enough, but one may suppose that they do not quarrel with their bread and butter (for it means that) out of sheer wantonness. In Ireland we have the strange paradox that while no nation perhaps produces, in proportion to population, so large a number of gifted writers, in no nation is the writer so neglected, when he is not harried and denounced. And yet, as I have said, I believe that a respect for the craft of letters is instinctive in the Irish common man—possibly even since the time when, as some chronicles affirm, the population was chiefly composed of professional bards.

In the year 1924, shortly after those upheavals in which so many Irishmen had died for what they supposed to be freedom, a journal appeared in Dublin which was regarded by the Irish Catholic press and public with no friendly eye. Its publication had in fact to be discontinued after the second number. In any other European country at that time it would have amused by its old-world pietism—the contributions ranged from dialectics rather in the manner of Maritain to short stories which might have been written by a youthful Mauriac. The paper was headed by a manifesto, plainly from the pen of Ireland's greatest poet, but signed collectively by a number of the contributors. As it seems to me of sufficient interest to be worth salvaging from oblivion, I make bold to reproduce it in full. With some reserves, I still think it almost a Scripture for Irish youth; and I am proud to believe that words of such authority could perhaps now only be written (though not, alas, printed!) in Ireland:—

We are Catholics, but of the school of Pope Julius II and of the Medicean Popes, who ordered Michelangelo and Raphael to paint upon the walls of the Vatican, and upon the ceiling of the Sistine Chapel, the doctrine of the Platonic Academy of Florence, the reconciliation of Galilee and Parnassus. We proclaim Michelangelo the most orthodox of men, because he set upon the tombs of the Medici "Dawn" and "Night", vast forms shadowing the strength of antediluvian Patriarchs and the lust of the goat, the whole handiwork of God, even the abounding horn.

We proclaim that we can forgive the sinner, but abhor the atheist, and that we count among atheists bad writers and bishops of all denominations (*sic*). "The Holy Spirit is an intellectual fountain", and, did the bishops believe, that Holy Spirit would show itself in decoration and architecture, in daily manners and written style. What devout man can read the pastorals of our Hierarchy without horror at a style rancid, coarse and vague, like that of the daily papers? We condemn the art and literature of modern Europe. No man can create, as did Shakespeare, Homer, Sophocles, who does not believe, with all his blood and nerve, that man's soul is immortal, for the evidence lies plain to all men that where that belief has declined men have turned from creation to photography. We condemn, though not without sympathy, those who would escape from banal mechanism through technical investigation and experiment. We proclaim that these bring no escape, for new form comes from new subject-matter, and new subject-matter must flow from the human soul restored to all its courage, to all its audacity. We dismiss all demagogues and call back the soul to its ancient sovranty, and declare that it can do whatever it please, being made, as antiquity affirmed, from the imperishable substance of the stars.*

Apart from the unfortunate reference to the bishops (which was of course deliberately provocative), there is little in all this to which cultured Roman Catholics in other countries would object; and it is surely expressed in splendid language. But this manifesto—and kindred matter in the journal—caused a hubbub of which the reverberations have scarcely yet subsided. The signatories seemed oddly unaware that in Ireland to call a man (let alone a bishop!) an atheist is more resented than to attach to him any other conceivable abusive term— such as rogue, thief, murderer, etc. And yet they should have had understanding and even approval for this, since it is in the spirit of their own declaration ("We can forgive the sinner but abhor the atheist"). But then of course the signatories did not fully mean what they said. They were conscious of paradox—whereas real Irish Catholics judge as simply as their medieval forefathers would have judged.

To call the Irish bishops "atheists" (because their pastorals are not written, say, in the style of this manifesto!) is to use words in a way which only artists and poets, I am afraid, are likely to understand. I have written on the question elsewhere,† but, as it seems to me perhaps the most important of all questions at the present day, I cannot resist giving a few hints in regard to it here. The artist is the servant of irrational (or rather supralogical) intuitions—intuitions which, at their purest, can only be uttered through the medium of style, and not through that of mere factual statement. He has no need

* Reproduced from *Tomorrow* by permission of the Editors and of Mrs. W. B. Yeats.

† *The Twilight of the Ideas, and Other Essays* (Sandymount Press, Dublin).

—at least in the moments when he is truly an artist—for "systems of belief"; rather they get in his way, they seem to him irrelevant and inadequate to the object of his belief, so that he will often appear to be a mocker. He is, essentially, neither a Protestant nor a Catholic but a Gnostic. The Church's function, on the other hand, is to present supra-logical truth under the forms of fact and logic—to rationalise the supra-rational—for the apprehension of all men at all moments. Until this difference is understood, there can be nothing but cross-purposes between churchmen and artists—especially in this island of Saints and Bards. It is my personal conviction that the "reconciliation of Galilee and Parnassus"—that synthesis which was attempted prematurely and not very seriously by the Renascence Popes—must be the next great stage in the evolution of human thought, if humanity is to have any future at all. That I do not exaggerate its importance should be clear from the fact that the world, outside of Ireland, has almost ceased to listen to the priest, and has begun to listen—with dangerous lack of discrimination—to almost anyone who calls himself an artist. Sham-artists—of whom the evil mass-mesmerist Adolf Hitler is very much the type—are the heresiarchs of today. Ireland still holds on to the other tray of the balance, but at present she tries to tie it down.

Irish Catholics are not often, certainly, of the "school" of Julius II, or the Medici, or Alexander Borgia, but they are a little of the school of the Early Fathers and the Saints of the Desert. For they believe in mortifying the flesh—and are quite serious about it. I have read that many French Jansenist priests came to Ireland when Maynooth was looking for professors, and their distaste for the pleasant side of life no doubt found here a congenial climate. In 1925 a Dublin bricklayer named Matt Talbot fell dead on his way to Mass. When his clothes were removed before burial, it was found that a cart-chain was tied tightly round his body, hung with religious medals; other chains and ropes were twisted around his arms and legs. The body was in a state of perfect cleanliness, but the chains were rusted and had eaten into the flesh. For twelve years he had worn the chains, slept on planks with a wooden pillow, fasted rigorously, and made surprising donations to charity out of his wages as a bricklayer. He had apparently been popular with his workmates, and was in no way abnormal; in his youth he had been somewhat of an over-fervent devotee of Bacchus. When his carefully-concealed austerities were made known after his death, he was certainly not thought by anyone to have been queer or odd; to cast ridicule on Matt Talbot in a Dublin pub would be very definitely to look for trouble. "He was so full of the love of God"—I quote from the C.T.S. leaflet—"that he could not hide his feelings, and this on one or two occasions caused uneasiness to his friends lest it should lead to spiritual pride. One of them spoke to him openly on the point, and reminded him of the danger that existed for a man who had been so highly gifted with the spirit of prayer, lest he should feel any self-satisfaction in it. He listened without comment, and then answered that he could never think of the great Saints and feel pride in what he had done." This, mark you, is a conversation between Dublin workmen. One may think what one likes of ascetic practices, but a character such as Talbot cannot be dismissed with the easy epithet "masochistic". It seems probable that his beatification is only a matter of time, and that he will eventually take his place in the calendar as St. Matthew—though Rome has given the "Island of Saints" rather less than her due in the matter of canonisations.

Eire is not a very gay country to live in, but at least the

Irish masses are not—generally speaking—ignoble in their holiday amusements. They do not go to a Blackpool—they go to St. Patrick's Purgatory in Loch Derg; nor do they go there as trippers. Figure to yourself an island which might be taken out of Leonardo's picture "The Madonna of the Rocks" but for being perpetually drenched in mist or lashed with rain. Here every "season" many thousands of pilgrims, of both sexes and of every class and trade, crawl and stumble on bare and bleeding knees up steep, slippery places, meditating as they do so on the successive stages (or "stations") of the Passion of Christ. For three days long they repeat and again repeat this dolorous performance—three days during which all their fare consists in a single meal daily of dry bread and water or black tea. Their first night is passed in a "Vigil" in the Basilica, after they have stood in turn with their backs to the Cross of St. Bridget, their arms outstretched, and thrice renounced the World, the Flesh and the Devil. If anyone should feel inclined to scoff at all this, let him go and consider the modern masses at their pleasures. I personally am one of those who believe in making oneself as comfortable as circumstances will permit; but if I had to choose between Loch Derg and Blackpool, I should choose Loch Derg without a moment's hesitation.

. . . . . .

This leads us to a discussion of the famous Irish chastity, which has been the subject of a certain amount of cant on the one side and of unjust accusations of hypocrisy on the other. A chapter certainly needs to be written on "The Sexual Life of the Irish", but, as I do not particularly want to be banned, it will not be written here. Moreover he would be an exceptionally sharp observer and deep psychologist who would be able to write it at all; for to all appearance the Irish really have

no sexual life, beyond the minimum necessary to per-
petuate their cantankerous species. The Irish coldness of
temper is older, certainly, than Queen Victoria, older than
Jansenius, older I think than St. Patrick; for it is an almost
uncanny natural innocence, and not (like English puritan-
ism) a matter of social discipline. If the English language
is a dull and harsh medium for love-making, the Gaelic
vocabulary of passion is often (to my ear) infantile and
uncouth; the Irish word for "kiss" is *póg*—the gesture of
pug-lips—the word for "love" is the hideous *grá*—a
rattle in the throat. There is an Irish proverb that the
rain has caused the death of every Irishman; and it would
seem as if it had also a little watered down the Irish blood.
But the habit of tracing national characters to climatic
causes is certainly "too easy"; every spiritual fact has a
thousand material roots, and a fear of all intense physical
or gregarious life seems to have been native to the Irish
from the earliest times—it is shown even in the peculiar
aversion of the old Gaels to living in towns. There is
coarse and rustic *grotesquerie* in the Gaelic mythology, but
there is very little passion; the *Táin*, the great Irish
Iliad, celebrates a raid for the recovery of a bull, not for
gaining possession of a woman. Doubtless the bull—like
the goat still annually exhibited on a platform at Puck
Fair in Kerry—is a totem with obvious significations;
but at least those significations seem never to have been
clearly present to the mind. So accessible, apparently,
was the hero Cuchulainn to the emotion of modesty, that
to calm his battle-fury and make him cover his face it was
only necessary to send forward naked women to meet
him. Even if this is a mere instance of the potency of a
tabu (I have read that the same technique was employed
in Ancient Ireland for purposes of ambuscade), the existence of the implied tabu is itself sufficiently remarkable.
In the Gaelic love-romances (as in the plays of Shaw) the

woman alone seems to evince passion. The male is a characterless, wailing and complaining figure, acting not from the heat of the blood but in conformity with a destiny mysteriously laid on him by spells and oracles—the exact prototype of the Irish lover of today, who is never done cursing his fate, and is quick to heap the most ungallant reproaches on his partner. Does not the anthem called "St. Patrick's Breastplate" invoke divine protection against the spells of "women, smiths and druids"? When Diarmuid and Gráinne in the course of their elopement happen to cross a ford, and the water splashes above Gráinne's knee, she says jibingly to Diarmuid "The water has more courage than you have". So it was then—so it is today; the Irish husband and father does not need to go in fear of the professional Don Juan—nor, on the other hand, does one notice the charming and gallant relations that one so often sees on the Continent between man and wife. The very words for brother and sister in Gaelic, if used simply and without prefix, mean always "monk" and "nun". In Ireland the conversion of the people to Christianity—elsewhere a slow and bitter process— seems to have come like a spontaneous joyous awakening from the age-long Druidic dream; and, having once discovered the Catholic faith, they have never shown the slightest inclination to depart from it. The Irish are not only *animae naturaliter Christianae*, but they are almost natural Manicheans; for them the World, the Flesh and the Devil are really interchangeable terms; as I have read in some German occult literature, that remnant of the ancient Atlantis called Hibernia has escaped—at least Ireland would fervently like to have escaped—from the consequences of the Fall. The case is only strengthened by a consideration of the one vice to which Irishmen are undoubtedly prone—I mean their drunkenness. The Irishman takes his drinking sadly; it is like a mournful symbol that even his beer is black. He drinks to attain forget-fulness of the whole human condition—that condition to which he feels himself so exceedingly ill-adapted.

Whether or no I am correct in the above analysis, it remains true that the most exacting standard of Christian morality is enforced in Ireland, not only by the law but—which is far more important—by the full weight of public opinion. To anyone accustomed to the easier atmosphere of other countries, it cannot be denied that Irish social life seems a little lacking in warmth and sparkle; but there is certainly no hypocrisy about it. A good-looking Austrian youth once described to me, with comic despair, how his hopes had been raised by the engaging friendli-ness of Irish female acquaintances, only to be as quickly dashed when he tried to improve the acquaintance. "I was quite bowled over" he said "the first time that I received the answer 'Irishwomen don't do that'. If the girl had replied 'I don't do that' I should have known how to deal with it." A young man in Irish cities does not meet with those casual brushes and glances which set the fancy on fire. On the other hand, the famous "Irish eyes"—whether or not they are like "a morn in Spring" as the sentimental song says—usually regard one with a frank and humorous expression which, to an unspoilt taste, can be extremely attractive.

The purity-cult of the Irish people, a matter of legitimate pride to themselves, is usually a subject for bitter derision to the intellectuals, who—like intellectual classes everywhere—are inclined to favour an unre-strained hedonism, at least in theory. I think there is in-deed something a little wrong with the Irish—especially the Irish *men*—but I doubt whether the intellectuals put the blame quite in the right place. It cannot be too often repeated that sexual freedom generally turns out to be hard on women—if not materially (not, at least, in countries such as the U.S.A., where the instinct of chivalry is strong), then certainly psychologically. If, as the feminists are so fond of telling us, the home is the woman's prison, it is perhaps also her castle. The real bane of Irish life is not the lack of libertinism but the late marriages—a feature noticed even in the more cheerful days of the 18th Century, and satirised in that finest of modern Gaelic poems *The Midnight Court*.* The average marrying age in Ireland for both sexes is something over thirty, and a surprising proportion of Irish men and women pass their whole lives not only celibate but (I honestly believe) as chaste as their own priests and nuns. This is really overdoing it—one cannot but feel that such people need the attention of specialists or dieteticians. I think it is fair to say that the average Irishman does not regard getting married as a normal, more or less inevitable, proceeding; he regards it as a possible—though rather desperate—means to "bettering" oneself, or else as a luxury, only safely to be indulged in *after* one has bettered oneself. As for falling in love, that seems to him the very height of absurdity; in no respect is the Protestant Shaw closer to his namesake, the Catholic Joyce,† than in their—typically Irish—titter over amorous infatuation. I have known Irishmen to act foolishly or dementedly from many causes, but seldom or never from the pang of Cupid's dart. Their attitude, at its finest, is well expressed in Padraic Colum's poem (a translation from medieval Gaelic),

> O woman shapely as the swan,
> On your account I shall not die!

---

* The excellent translation by Frank O'Connor (Fridberg 1945) is banned in Eire. An earlier translation by the present writer (not banned, by some oversight) is out of print. The original Gaelic text is also long out of print, so that Irishmen have now no means of acquainting themselves with the best poem of their language.

† Shaw and Joyce are both Anglicisms for the Gaelic *Seogh*. Shaw is the Scottish form.

It is often said that Irish parish priests forbid courtship; what is perhaps more to the point is that a country youth who showed any of the tender feeling would be regarded as "astray in his wits" and become the butt of the local humorists—he and his sweetheart would suffer the disgusting indignities to which Parnellite candidates were treated after the tragic and touching affair of Kitty O'Shea. All this means that ordinary Irish men and women (especially, I repeat, the men) give a rather distressing impression of immaturity, of social gawkiness and sheepishness, of physical uncouthness and *malaise*. In rural Ireland they are called "boys" and "girls" for as long as they continue in a dependent relation to their parents (often, that is to say, till late in life); and adolescents in appearance and character many Irish people in fact remain, until withering into a premature and vaguely unsatisfied old age. If the late Mrs. Shaw intended, by her extraordinary last will and testament, to endow an Irish school of gallantry, I would certainly agree that "no nation needed it so much"; the more so as an interest in the gay science might lead to an improvement—much needed—in the related sciences of dress and food. (The fact—to take one instance among many—that our agricultural country can boast no fine native *cheese* is simply deplorable.) As an extremely intelligent English lady, living in Ireland, once said to me "Most Irishmen are content to curse women and leave it at that. They are sexually maladjusted, and ease themselves by improprieties and incivilities." It is this, I think, and not the praiseworthy good-living of the Irish, which is aesthetically unpleasing in their "purity"—a purity which at the same time has given us the peculiar cold beauty of Gaelic myths and nature-poetry. It is possible that in this respect Latin Christianity (especially of the later, rather morbid, Jansenist type) has really been bad for us—has substituted a factitious chastity for a real and very unique innocence.

I cannot here avoid touching on the question of the Censorship—a very sore subject indeed with Irish men of letters. So indignant do they feel about it (often, certainly, on very just personal grounds) that they seem to lose all sense of proportion when discussing the Infamous Thing; they speak of it as if it were a scandal and a tyranny which restores the empire of Old Night as though by Chaos's uncreating hand. Their enthusiasm for Liberty would be creditable enough, were it not that so many of them admire systems of government which would strip us of every shred of liberty that we still possess. The question of censorship is in fact not so simple. After all, nobody today believes in liberty quite in the way that John Stuart Mill believed in it, except perhaps some of the older members of the Reform Club in Pall Mall; we no longer trust our fellow-men enough for that. Milton, it is true, advanced some excellent reasons against censorship; but in Milton's day very few people could read, and a free printing-press was not likely to be more harmful than the fact that gentlemen could carry swords. The arrival (regrettable, one so often feels) of popular education has entirely altered the dimensions of the problem. And here I should point out that the Irish Censorship Board is not—as many people in England seem to imagine—a council of cowled inquisitors, assembled to root out heretical opinions; it is a committee of laymen, on which Protestants are duly represented, and the only "heresy" which it suppresses is the neo-Malthusian one. (*Crux Ansata*, H. G. Wells' crude attack on the Catholic Church, was allowed to circulate freely in Eire.) Apart from that debatable matter, the Censorship is instituted to suppress obscenity and indecency—surely (one would at first sight imagine) an unexceptionable aim, and an attempt to deal with what is, as every educationist knows, a very real abuse in all civilised cities. Those who maintain that nobody would read pornographic rubbish anyway, "because it is so dull", are, I think, a trifle over-optimistic. No one who travelled in pre-Hitler Germany can doubt that the pathological excesses later associated with the concentration camps were due, in no small measure, to the deluge of pseudo-medical literature (profusely illustrated) to which the post-War German youth was exposed—dealing almost entirely with sexual perversions, and sold on every bookstall. (Was there not a story of an English Quaker who bought a copy of the paper called *Der Freund*, under the slight misapprehension that it was the organ of the Society of Friends?)

Thus far the Speech for the Defence; but there is, alas, another side to the matter. The Irish Censorship is in fact as lamentable in its operation as it is praiseworthy in its presumable intention. Glancing down the list of writers to whom the Censors have, at one time or another, pinned the insulting label "obscene and indecent", one's eyes open in wonder and astonishment as one comes upon the following names: G. B. Shaw (!), Charles Morgan, Christopher Morley, Richard Aldington, Wyndham Lewis, T. F. Powys (and all the other Powyses), Thomas Mann (and Heinrich Mann), Stefan Zweig, Erich Maria Remarque, Romain Rolland, André Malraux, Henry de Montherlant, Stephen Spender, Robert Graves, J. Middleton Murry, Bonamy Dobrée, Henri Barbusse, Scholem Asch, Mikhail Sholokhov, Maxim Gorki, Theodore Dreiser, Ernest Hemingway, Aldous Huxley (almost all works), Somerset Maugham (his beautiful *Cakes and Ale*), L. A. G. Strong, Storm Jameson, Eleanor Farjeon, Compton Mackenzie, Graham Greene, A. J. Cronin, etc., etc. (The last three are, as everyone knows,

D

distinguished Catholic intellectuals, and they are not the only ones on the list.) Also the name of practically every living Irish writer of international repute.

This is simply a joke, and it would be a mistake to treat it too solemnly, especially as the Censors cannot really keep the works of these authors from people who want them. Anyone who truly regards the above-named writers as purveyors of filth must be of the mental age of a schoolboy—and a dull and unpleasant schoolboy at that. If these authors are indecent they are so in the same sense as are Shakespeare and Ariosto and the Bible and *The Brothers Karamazov* and the old folk-songs and what you will—because literature happens to be concerned with the whole of reality. Aldous Huxley's *Brave New World* (banned) is a work which every Catholic theologian should have on his bookshelf—a devastating satire on materialistic hedonism and all the modern attempts to reconstruct the Earthly Paradise, a book that—but for its cold violence—might have been written by G. K. Chesterton. I wonder which of the two is the luckier that Swift is not alive today—he or the Censorship Board?

And now let us turn from the serious and sincere writers who have had the misfortune to incur the Censors' displeasure to a sort of literature which enjoys almost unimpeded circulation in Eire.

I stroll out from my house to the "Forget-me-not Library"—one of those smaller circulating libraries which are to be found at most street-corners, where the servant-girl can get her weekly thrill for the modest charge of 3d (and 2s 6d deposit). I turn over the well-thumbed pages of works with such titles as *The Hesitating Nymph, Her One Lapse*, or *Love on the Lido*; but I do not have to turn over very many before I meet with the following lively description:

She heard with beating heart the sound of approaching footsteps. Never had she so detested a man, yet she felt utterly powerless to prevent his entering her room. With a kind of hypnotised horror she saw the handle turn and the door swing open. Drawing her flimsy negligee closer about her, she attempted to still the chattering of her teeth. He stood before her.

"I told you to be ready when I called," he said.

"I won't be ordered about like that." She tried to speak boldly, but her voice sank to a dry whisper as he advanced upon her with that detestable smile still on his face.

"Get ready, you little fool," he snarled.

As he gripped her arms with his powerful fingers she felt the strength drain from her limbs. Her knees seemed to turn to water. The room swam round her.

"Yes," she stammered incoherently.

He crushed her trembling body to him with one arm. With the other he reached out behind him, and switched off the light. . . .

It is fair to say that the Censors keep out a certain amount of literature of this class; but they (or the officious persons who send them up the books, with marked passages) are, by an instinctive bias, more on the alert for works like Kate O'Brien's wonderful *Land of Spices* than for the novelettes of the cheaper bookstalls. What conclusion are we to draw from all this? Simply (or so it would seem) that the Censorship is maintained, primarily, for the purpose of baiting the intellectuals. It is a pity, for I should like to have seen my country show the world a really fine example of Censorship and How to Do it. It is a problem which will have to be tackled some day by every free democracy, and Ireland has the incomparable advantage that she still recognises a spiritual authority and the necessity for specialists in the field of morals. But, unfortunately, Irishmen have sung for so long the line of Thomas Davis "for righteous men must make our land a nation once again" that they have forgotten that *cultured* men should also have a say. And righteousness without culture has a tendency to turn rancid.

I cannot leave this subject without adding that, of course, I understand the Censors very well, and—to a point—I sympathise with them; they are trying to keep out the anarchy and the lack of standards which is the canker of modern life. They do not (as they profess) attempt to exclude the greatest living masters of literature because they are indecent or obscene. They ban them because they sense in them a non-Catholic (what they would call a "Pagan") mentality, which if it were allowed to increase and establish itself in Eire would end in producing immoral customs—as it does elsewhere; and they sense this mentality even in some famous Roman converts. They do not *so* much mind the pornography of the gutter, so long as the traditional labels "sin" and "virtue" do not get mixed up; the ribald but essentially Catholic James Joyce remains uncensored in his native country.* What they fear is the thing which the Protestant W. B. Yeats also condemned—though in a malicious paradox—namely "atheism". This is a quite understandable position, though the fact that it is not—perhaps could not be—frankly admitted creates an atmosphere of disingenuousness, and leads to such laughable results as those we have noted. Nevertheless one may wonder, after all is said, whether the Irish are not guided by a right instinct in so obstinately refusing the modern siren-voices.

* Needless to say, I do not mean to imply any assimilation of Joyce to the gutter-literature.

Refusal, refusal—that is the key-word to the Irish character; Ireland is the Old Lady who always says No. The Irish, as I know them, are not a race of haters, they are not unforgiving; what has always impressed me most is their gentle tolerance—a tolerance like that of women and priests. A deputy, whose life had been attempted, sought out his would-be assassin, saying he felt sure they would be friends. The Irishman's venom is canalised off in swearing or speech-making or malicious conversation —all three of which accomplishments he has brought to a high pitch of cultivation. (There has perhaps been lately some falling-off in the standard of Irish oratory; yet I heard a very second-rank Irish politician address a dinner-table of notables in Amsterdam, and he moved them to the verge of tears.) The Irish "war of liberation" was fought without real hate; there were no murderous attacks on the loyalists; the Great Famine—almost the greatest horror of the civilised 19th Century, occurring amidst abundant crops—left surprisingly little rancour behind it, at least among those who remained in the fatalistic air of Ireland. It is not the "long memory" of the Irish (an academic, almost unimpassioned, thing) which prevents them loyally taking their place in the Empire; it is simply that they feel themselves elder children of another, invisible, Empire—they whose missionaries largely Christianised Northern Europe in the Dark Ages, and who are Catholicising the English-speaking world today. In the cheerful, pedestrian materialism of the British—their mundane moral earnestness—their full-blooded omnivorous acceptance of life—in all this there is something deeply antipathetic to the Irish temper. Ireland with her population of three millions feels as indestructible, as confident in her destiny, as England feels with her forty-three millions. If Europe should be submerged by the wave of Asiatic

Communism, will North America become the Catholic continent of the next century? Will her Catholicism be Irish rather than Italian or French in character? It is very possible. Indeed, if one wishes to indulge in a patriotic fancy, one may even imagine the Christian culture coming back to paganised Europe, not by means of American atom-bombs, but once again through the Irish monks.

Refusal, repression, escape; the Irishman is the born introvert—for evil, but also for good. His gentle speech and manners are defensive, not expansive; and they are liable suddenly to fail, giving place, rather disconcertingly, to violent vituperation. The poorest Englishman will declare "I speaks my mind." An Irishman will say "So-and-so is a bold man—he says out what's in his mind"; and in Ireland, as in the nursery, the word "bold" is used in a pejorative sense. A farmer admitted to my grandfather, speaking of Home Rule, "We're all for it collectively, but we're all against it individually." But indeed an Irishman usually has to be drunk or under anaesthetics before you can catch him without his slightly mocking inscrutability. One may put the matter cruelly and say the Irishman is always afraid—afraid of his thoughts, his desires, his neighbours. Or one may put it kindly and say that his pride or his fastidiousness are forever holding him back—that he remains disdainfully ironical before sensual passion or communal purpose. At his best he is like some mad king of legend, in a world of tamed, groomed citizens; at his worst he suggests some rather malevolent gnome from the roots of the hills. There is in him something of great Jonathan Swift—but also something of Swift's distorted double, the vision that rotted his brain, the Yahoo. How often Irish faces are refined and noble—only something is wrong: the eyes are too wide apart and do not seem to focus, or the nose

(even in a peasant) is that of some more-than-decadent
Bourbon. My Irish readers will reply at once with those
"seven hundred years of slavery"; only I have a feeling
that if I were to meet Suibhne Gealt or the Giolla
Deacair, or any of the strange and twisted characters that
people Irish mythology, they would look very much the
same. Photographers will understand me when I say
that in the Irish scene there is a diffused and glowing light,
but little of solidity or definition; and it is somewhat the
same, I think, with the face and mind of Ireland.
"Brightness falls from the air"—and falls on pools of
bog-water. The Irishman lives by preference in Eternity, among the legends—Pagan or Christian—avoiding
the tumults and the tragedies of Time; his soul, when
one touches it, is proud and pure, but everything else
about him seems restricted and timid. Curiously, by a
sort of polarisation, the Irish woman often seems to be a
virago, earthy and passionate and very male—like Queen
Maeve, or the 16th-Century pirate-chieftainess Grace
O'Malley, or Synge's heroine Pegeen Mike. Ireland is a
country of great fighting mothers—of Junos, like the one
in O'Casey's play, but not, certainly, of Jupiters.

The Irish mind has irony, and it has the mystical
sense; but I think (paradox though it may sound) that
it has little real understanding for moral or even for
tragic feeling. An Irishman cannot really take morality
seriously, as a good in itself like religion or beauty; for
him it is either the book of the rules for getting to heaven,
or a matter of personal fastidiousness. If that seems to an
English reader to be selfish, I can only reply that to us
(rightly or wrongly) it is utilitarian ethics which seem
like glorified self-interest. I do not know if Irish boy-
scouts try to do a good action every day; but if they do so,
it must be purely in the spirit of a ritual observance.
And equally, I think, there is something slightly uncon-

vincing about Irish heroics—even when hallowed by a quasi-religious tradition. I once read an essay by Giovanni Papini in which he sought to prove that Don Quixote was not really a tragic figure but a literary poseur—it was the credulous Sancho who was tragic; and I think the theory might be applied with some truth to the Irish Quixotes. Ireland's patriotic songs (some of which I have, a little irreverently, quoted) are, unlike those of the Scots, almost all conventional and bad; but her street-ballads, like "The Night before Larry was Stretched" or "When I was Going to Sweet Athy", are brutal and fine—with a hint of tenderness that would perhaps be missed by any but Irish ears. I have already spoken of the Irish insensibility to romantic love, but is there another country in which a soldier's sweetheart would thus apostrophise her sadly-mauled gallant, home from the wars:

> You haven't an arm and you haven't a leg,
> You're an eyeless, noseless, chickenless egg,
> You'll have to be put in a bowl to beg—
>   O Johnnie I hardly knew you!
>
> Where are the legs with which you run
> When first you went to carry a gun?
> Indeed your dancing-days are done—
>   O Johnnie I hardly knew you!
>
> Where are the eyes that looked so mild, etc.

When W. B. Yeats refused to include even one of the powerful and moving war-poems of Wilfred Owen in his *Oxford Book of Modern Verse*, he caused (justifiably I think) some indignation in England; but Owen's pathos and humanity meant nothing to Yeats. "He had not been in the trenches" you will say; and it is undeniable that the savage flippancy and amoralism of Irishmen are the marks of a rather simple society, in which good and evil have not yet become extremely serious matters; if the Yeatsian philosophy had grown (for instance) on German soil, it could hardly have helped developing into Nazi diabolism. Nothing is more revealing than the way in which Yeats celebrates vagabonds and sluts if one compares it with the way in which English poets glorify the same characters. The latter will never fail to suggest that the man is a noble fellow under his rags, or that the woman is really more sinned against than sinning; whereas Yeats is stressing that all of us are rogues or sluts beneath the varnish.

To the Irishman's instinct (if I see him rightly) the real sin, the only tragedy, is being born; he would understand the words of the old mystic "Most specially he feeleth matter of sorrow that knoweth and feeleth that he is". Such metaphysical intuitions can perhaps only be expressed in music; Gaelic folk-music is unspeakably sad, but most Gaelic literature is formal, patterned and almost passionless. Just because the Irish are close to elemental sorrow, they are apt to see little but the ridiculous side of private and particular passions and tragedies. There is much more of laughter than horror in Irish myths and fairy-tales; there are few dragons or wicked stepmothers; there is almost nothing of the Teutonic (or even the Classical) sense of Doom and Dread. It seems, indeed, a world before the Fall. It is here that the literature and folklore of the Scottish Gaels show the most complete contrast to that of their Irish parent-stock; just as the life of Ireland was gentler than the Scottish life, with its witch-burnings and savage feuds. There can be nothing more ghastly than some of the Scottish Border-Ballads; but for that very reason, perhaps, they are better poetry in their kind than anything the more lily-livered Irish ever wrote. Like all religious peoples, Irishmen regard existence rather as a puppet-show; the afflicted ladies by whose names 18th-Century bards allegorise their country are generally too hieratic and conventional to be really moving. A farmer of my acquaintance refused to let his daughter's hair be cut during a dangerous fever, though he was told it might be the one chance of saving her life; should she die, he said, she would not make such a nice corpse without her hair. The Irishman likes the priest because the priest seems to him not quite human, and he wants his leaders to be—like the Pope or the Grand Cham—remote, scornful, almost inaccessible. Nothing, for instance, could make less of an appeal to him than the popular monarchy of the British—or, for that matter, the extremely *häuslich* little princes and princesses of Grimms' Fairy Tales. An Irish leader must be so individual that he is mysterious and almost legendary while he is still alive; whereas an English king must be so much of a public institution that he almost ceases to have any individuality at all. The English sentiment about royalty has been wickedly satirised in the lines:

> A stone, a piece of orange-peel,
> The end of a cigar,
> If trod on by a royal heel
> How beautiful they are!

For the Englishman, it would seem, it is the Crown, and not the possession of any personal qualities, that makes the King—the more so as he is not expected actually to rule; but the King is interesting only because he is alive and "in the news", the lynch-pin of the whole mighty engine of Real Life, a practical and functioning entity. English Constitutional Monarchy is perhaps the finest product of the unrivalled English political genius. But the Irishman is a natural Jacobite—he prefers uncrowned kings. Moreover, unlike the Scottish Jacobite, he would keep them uncrowned; he would not submit them to the test of reality. A real Irish king, sceptred and gartered, would seem to the Irishman ridiculous, and probably would be ridiculous—a sort of glorified Dublin Lord Mayor. Most of all your Irishman likes his kings dead; the only Irish pomps are *pompes funèbres*. I do not wish to be an augur of untoward events; but one's breath fails at the thought of the funeral that Ireland will one day give to Eamonn De Valera.

This may help to explain that baffling matter of Ireland's attitude to the Gaelic. Almost everyone in Eire now has a smattering of Irish; it would seem to need only one Grand Resolution to make it the living speech of the country tomorrow; but that resolution—one feels certain—will never be made, and the vernacular is in fact seldom heard outside those few and remote parishes where the English language never established itself. The Gaelic is taught in practically every school, primary or secondary, and in very many classes it has been made the sole vehicle of all instruction—with not very happy results for the sciences which have to be filtered through this archaic medium by a teacher whose mother-tongue is English to an English-speaking class. The consequence, it is not too much to say (though I should hesitate as an anti-modern to call this an unmitigated misfortune), has been a most serious setback to education in Eire. But the gain, so far as the revival of Gaelic is concerned, is precisely nil; worse than that, it has made the "Compulsory Irish" as heartily hated throughout the length and breadth of the republic as was ever the tongue of the conqueror. But this must be said with an important reserve. The Irish of course like their Irish, but they like it *dead*, and as far as possible both useless and unused. They want it preserved as a symbol—an heirloom testifying to their ancient racial lineage; but they do not really want it debased to the prosaic purposes of modern daily living— purposes for which, moreover, they know it to be ill-adapted. And it cannot unfortunately be kept as a

literary language, because there happens to be almost
no literature in post-medieval Irish much worth bother-
ing about; its literature still waits to be written—if, as the
patriots rather pathetically pretend to believe, a Gaelic
literature today is conceivable. The Irishman is in practical affairs very much of a realist and even a "material-
ist"; he knows that the Gaelic is a sad nuisance and
handicap to his children (some of whom will most probably have to earn their livings outside of Ireland); but
so necessary to him is this symbol of his separate national
being that he seems unable to do anything about his
"Compulsory Irish" Green Elephant. The last generation in Ireland really killed their ancestral tongue (refusing to speak it in their homes, for sensible-enough
practical reasons) rather in the same way as they killed
their great but disgraced chief Parnell; but, just as they
sometimes dreamed of a return of the lost leader, so they
dreamed—and their children still dream—of a "come-
back" of the murdered language, while not really be-
lieving in it or hoping for it. It is an interesting example
of our national talent for making the worst of both
worlds—the natural result of our refusal to live completely in the only world which we (at present)
have.

In all this I do not mean to sneer. I too gave my first
love to the Gaelic, among languages; and my conclusions
are based, not on any sour study of my countrymen, but
largely on an examination of my own complex feelings.
My relations to this distressed heroine, to be endurable,
must be somewhat platonic; but I do not wish to drop her
completely. It was an ancestor of my own, John Ussher,
who in 1571 published the first book printed in Gaelic, a
translation of the Protestant Catechism; and his son, Sir
William Ussher, who was responsible for the first Irish
version of the New Testament, published in 1602—that

of William O'Donnell—to combat (as the Dedication explains) "the subtiltie of Antichrist and his vassals, the filthy frye of Romish seducers, the hellish firebrands of all our troubles". An interest in the language is therefore for me almost a case of *noblesse oblige*; and I have myself brought out (though from somewhat different motives—sponsored indeed by that fine scholar the late Dr. Sheehan, Catholic Archbishop of Melbourne) a two-volume anthology of the traditional speech of my neighbourhood. The way out of the language-dilemma is really simple if the right steps are taken at once—of which, however, there seems to be little or no prospect; it is, it seems to me, the obvious course to adopt with all such vernaculars, fated to be swept away by the giant besoms of press and radio. The Gaelic is, as I have said, a language without a modern literature, but it is a language of prodigious diversity of sound and expressiveness of phrase. Owing to its peculiar anatomy of "broad", "slender", "aspirated" and "eclipsed" consonants, it has about twice the number of sounds that other European languages can boast; sounds, too, for most of which there are no precise equivalents in any other tongue. (For instance: d broad is dth, d slender is dy, d aspirate broad is a sort of gargle, d aspirate slender is almost y, d eclipsed broad is an n with clenched teeth, d eclipsed slender is ny. There is no d as we know it in English, French, German etc.; and so with the other consonants.) The softening and eclipsing of initial consonants (according to complicated and uncertain rules) cause the words to dissolve and change their shapes like objects in a mist; more than with most languages, the student has to speak and think in unit-sentences rather than unit-words, as it were single indivisible spasms of feeling or imagination; "the colours run" on the palette—or the palate—so that he is lost if he has not a fine ear and a mobile larynx. As for the expressiveness of the Gaelic folk-idiom, only the "Irish English" of Synge's plays can give strangers some idea of it; it is the language, if not of a race of poets (perhaps we are too poetical to be poets, as Wilde said), then at least of a race which has "tired the sun with talking", a language of quips, hyperboles, cajoleries, lamentations, blessings, curses, endearments, tirades—and all very often in the same breath; but not a language into which you could easily translate, say, the *Encyclopædia Britannica*. Of all this richness, needless to say, one finds little enough trace in the synthetic, dehydrated, Gaelic of the classroom—the "refaned" equivalent of the French of Stratford-atte-Bowe. In ten years, or even in five, the last of the old traditional speakers will have gone to join Scott's Last Minstrel; the Irish which captivated the youthful George Borrow will be an indistinct memory, and there will remain only the Civil Service *Ersatz*—ill-pronounced, unidiomatic, and refurbished (to the confusion of every nuance) in the crude new official spelling. In these circumstances, why oh why is not an oral "library" founded in the capital, an Aeolian cave of voices, where the student could turn up in the catalogue the dialect and subject of his choice and be handed the appropriate phonograph records—with a printed translation—bottles, as it were, preserving for a more leisured posterity the flavour and "body" of the old indigenous speech? The Irish, lifted from the mires in which it is so fast disappearing, would become—not indeed, what no one really desires, as common as the stones of the roads—but treasured like the Crown-Jewels of the State, as every good Irishman would like to see it. This seems to me a cogent—and frightfully urgent—solution of a weary problem (a solution which I have already pressed for repeatedly in print, without effect); but the Compulsory Irish has now become a vested interest, and is likely to vex our tempers and befog our brains for many a long day.

The Irish coldness, to which I have made reference, must not be confused for a moment with British "phlegm". The characters of men and nations can perhaps nowhere be seen more revealingly than in their demeanour, on the one hand towards death, and on the other towards the female sex. It need hardly be said that for the English any clamorous expression of grief or sorrow is the very height of bad form. It is treason to the great cause of *Life*, it is helping to diffuse alarm and despondency, it is the crime of "letting down the side". In the words of Masefield (which fall flat enough on Irish ears) "Laugh and be proud to belong to the old proud pageant of man". An Englishman, lately informed that his whole family have perished in some disaster, will assume the mask-like expression of a Japanese Samurai—England and the dead themselves would expect it of him; at the most he will nervously bite his moustaches, as if he should never have been bothered with such a trifle. If he is really well-trained, he will attempt to continue the conversation or get on with the job in hand at the exact point he had reached when he was interrupted; and woe betide you if you should offer him your sympathy! The Icelandic warrior who remarked coolly, as he withdrew a spear-head from his vitals, "I knew these broad blades would soon be coming into fashion" was surely the first Englishman. But your average Englishman is not at all reserved about his amorousness; he pats, he twinkles, he cuddles, he chuckles—all with an expression of the most benign self-satisfaction. The behaviour of an English crowd on a bank-holiday is as distasteful, at first viewing, to the Irish of all classes as it is to cultured English folk. For it is hardly too much to say that the Irishman treats sex as the Englishman treats death. An Irishman on his "walks-out" (if he gets so far as that) will wear a look of the most studied boredom; while terrified of privacy, he will be careful—in any place the least public—to appear totally unconcerned with his companion. The proverbial remark of the Irish swain during an amorous encounter, "Take your ease, Mary, while I have a few pulls of my pipe", is scarcely an exaggeration. Far different is the attitude of the Irish to bereavement! Here they display (or used within very recent memory to display) a richness and splendour of feeling unequalled in any other Christian nation. The Irish wake of my boyhood, with the Gaelic dirge or "keen"—the flood of extempore poetry in a traditional rising-and-falling chant—was an event unique in its impressiveness. I will quote as an example, in rough translation, the lamentation of an ordinary plowman for his wife, which the man himself (by no means a sentimental character) repeated to me from memory; but I am conscious that it must sound bald indeed—and a little over-naïve—presented in the English clipped vowels, and without the modulations of the recitative:

O poor Josie, you are laid out now by the women, and there is fear upon my heart lest my tread should break your rest. And I have a strong belief that you are in the country of quiet now, but I shall never lay my eye till the butt of my life again on one who will break the ice like you. You used be at market and at fair with me, and indeed not like many another woman with your hood down over your eyes, but 'twas it that was fastened tightly at the back of your neck. It's well I remember the morning that the little man came from the South with the sweet tongue who thought to get the two calves from us for an old tune of Mary Bun; but, if he thought it, you put the fire in his coat-tails going, and you put the fleas jumping in the hair of the Kerryman. And it's well I remember the morning of the Christmas fair, when that other schemer came seeking the two fat pigs for the fasting-bite of a donkey; but, if he came, you put him in as much of a scurry as Red Beston was in the day he tried to pull his wife out from the band of the wheel, when she couldn't put a foot under her with drink, and fear was upon his heart that he'd be arrested by the peelers for putting her neck under the wheel himself. I never came in from the garden* to you but the little gate was open, the ass fed, and the little stirabout-pot ready beside the fire; but now the gate will be shut, the ass unfed, and the stirabout-pot on its mouth outside the door, and you'll never take a hold of the iron spoon again. And if anyone came short in their share it would be yourself, O woman of the great heart, and if the white goat ran dry the black goat didn't know it. You would play a tune on your tongue and dance to it, and maybe there would be puckers in your belly at the same time, and if there was another woman in your shoes it's often her husband wouldn't have the life of the black cat the day he didn't kill any rat. When the neighbour used come with the horse to plow up the garden for you, he used go out from you with his belly bursting, you used give him potatoes and salt pork and white cabbage, and you used give him a loaf and tea and a duck-egg, and you used give him the little quart of porter you had brought with you to be ready for the day you went to the market. He used be off then to the neighbours bellows-ing your praise, and he'd say that any poor man who had a good lucky wife, that his hen was on the nest and his rent in his pocket. And

---

* A cottage "garden" means a small tillage-field, usually a potato-patch.

now, my dear love, I must take your hand for the last moments—and I shall have to do it behind my back—for the poor women are here to settle you sweetly in your coffin, and you look so neat that you will be making cajolery up in the other world. And I see their heads bent, and the drop falling from their eyes, for they say they won't see a woman the like of you taking a clean shirt from the line ever again, for you never tore a rib of anyone's hair, and if you couldn't fill the cup you didn't spill it. But I see the blue light now shining on you, and as content as we always were I have a strong belief that you'll be a thousand times richer now possessing the Graces, for there won't be any itching on your mind to know where'll you get your breakfast on Easter Sunday morning. The angels will lay a soft bed for you, and you need have no fear that any wind will blow the little stack of barley out of the corner of the garden ever again. I will make the Sign of the Cross over you now between yourself and the Tempter, and God will direct you straight to the end of every crooked lane, into the strange Blessed Land—the place where the harvest is ready cut and threshed, and the barn filled to the top with the grain that will never fail.

This is, of course, the sorrow of the simple, though to my mind very nobly expressed, with the Biblical roll of its repetitions—its touches of half-conscious humour only serving to redeem it from monotony. As a sample of the more stately type of Irish dirge, I should like to quote Mangan's translation of "A Lament for the Knight of Kerry" by the 17th-Century Gaelic court-poet Ferriter (who was afterwards hanged)—a description of a concert of keening by the fairy-women, which in spite of the commonplaceness of Mangan's metre and "poetic diction" still conveys something of the Gaelic feeling:

There was lifted up one voice of woe,
  One lament of more than mortal grief,
Through the wide South to and fro,
  For a fallen chief.
In the dead of night that cry thrilled through me,
  I looked out upon the midnight air!
Mine own soul was all as gloomy,
  And I knelt in prayer.

O'er Loch Gur, that night, once—twice—yea, thrice—
  Passed a wail of anguish for the Brave
That half curdled into ice
  Its moon-mirroring wave.
Then uprose a many-toned wild hymn in
  Choral swell from Ogra's dark ravine,
And Mogeely's Phantom Women
  Mourned the Geraldine!

Far on Carah Mona's emerald plains
  Shrieks and sighs were blended many hours,
And Fermoy in fitful strains
  Answered from her towers.
Youghal, Keenalmeaky, Eemokilly,
  Mourned in concert, and their piercing keen
Woke to wondering life the stilly
  Glens of Inchiqueen.

From Loughmoe to yellow Dunanore
  There was fear; the traders of Tralee
Gathered up their golden store,
  And prepared to flee;
For, in ship and hall that night till morning
  Showed the first faint beamings of the sun,
All the foreigners heard the warning
  Of the Dreaded One!

"This" they spake "portendeth death to us,
  If we fly not swiftly from our fate!"
Self-conceited idiots! thus
  Ravingly to prate!
Not for base-born higgling Saxon trucksters
  Ring laments like those by shore and sea!
Not for churls with souls of hucksters
  Waileth our Banshee!

For the high Milesian race alone
  Ever flows the music of her woe!
For slain heir to bygone throne
  And for chief laid low!
Hark! . . . Again, methinks, I hear her weeping
  Yonder! Is she near me now, as then?
Or was't but the night-wind sweeping
  Down the hollow glen?

It is all a little artificial, at the best. In both of these cases, one knows, the mourner felt himself called upon to put out a really big effort; and certainly many Irish laments are as dismal and interminable as Irish funeral-processions. But if the Irish treat death with even excessive ceremony, they certainly do not believe in hushing it up.

.   .   .   .

I do not know if I have given the impression that life in Ireland is somewhat drab; drab, perhaps, is not altogether the right word. Ireland is a country in which the past turns quickly to legend, the future to mirage, and the present is a rather uncomfortable camping-place in the wilderness—uncomfortable or, if one is a natural Ishmaelite, exciting. The Irish are a little like the Jews—a race for whom I have always felt a warm sympathy—and the emigration during the 19th Century was a real dispersion; but, unlike the Jews, they have never lost contact with their Holy Land, and its peculiarly potent *genius loci*. Ireland, like Israel, has a sense of some special destiny, which enables her to bear her discomfitures with fatalism and secret pride. Some Catholic acquaintances of mine, "burnt out" by the British soldiery on Good Friday in 1920, were quite exalted by what they regarded an an extraordinary favour and privilege; it is unlikely that the soldiers realised they were accomplishing a religious rite. In Ireland one feels close to nature, to the other world, to the distant past—but there is, properly speaking, no *history*; no hungry generations tread one down, no laws have ever stopped the blades of grass from growing as they grow. The Irishman, like the nomad of the desert, has never built or reclaimed; he recklessly fells his trees and cuts away his turf, leaving nothing but naked mountain-side and soggy marsh—in spite of the recent pullulation of inspectors to control him—just as he has let his incomparable oral folk-tradition perish almost unrecorded.* He has constantly on his lips such sayings as "It's all equal", or "Ah what matter?", or the incontrovertible assertion "What will happen will happen and what will not happen will not happen". The Irish housewife congratulates herself on her wastefulness as much as a French housewife prides herself on her thrift. Such wastefulness also takes the form of spaciousness, and an almost noble claustrophobia; to enter the smallest Irish farm-house is to fancy oneself in a baron's hall, with its deep inglenooks on either side of the open hearth—its great central kitchen yawning to the rafters, and its upper bedrooms under the side-gables reached by ladders. The Irish in their own country never took kindly to towns, or even to villages. Every peasant carries the name of his "townland" like a title: Pat Rafferty of Mountain Castle, Matt Halloran of the Glen, Larry O'Murnaghan of Mullinahorna. One imagines a wide and thickly-populated country, only to find that each of these "townlands" comprises perhaps a score of acres, on which there may stand one small homestead. Ireland, I repeat, has no history, but she has a quite fascinating geography. In England a field is not a field, even if it has as yet escaped being built over—it is a place where a battle was fought, or a charter was signed, or if you dig deep enough you will possibly find a bit of Roman pavement. In England one never forgets the Roman arms and the Roman law. The British Empire seems as much a second birth of the Roman Empire, as the Irish seem like the race whose mysticism conquered Rome.

* Gratitude however is due to the work—little appreciated and handicapped by insufficient funds—of the Irish Folklore Commission, under the leadership of Séamas Ó Duilearga, which has already resulted in the accumulation of over a million pages of manuscript. But what can be saved is only the remnant of the Sybilline Books.

The Irish have this in common with the French, that
they have too much individualistic pride gladly to suffer
aristocracy or royalty; aristocracy, perhaps, can only
endure among truly democratic peoples like the British,
in whom "public spirit" is strong—even in the aristocrats. There is no rule that makes for stability so much as
rule by families; but such rule will not be tolerated in the
modern world if the upper castes are socially irrespon-
sible. The ancient Irish had no invariable succession
from father to son—a fact which accounts, more than any
other, for their failure to build a state that could resist the
British. The Irish "high-kings", like the priests of Nemi,
were mostly "assassinated by their successors", as one
may learn from a glance through the great patriotic
historian Keating; in theory, all Irish chieftains were—
within certain limits—elected, but one may imagine the
"election" was generally the acceptance of a *fait accompli*.
Such "elections" are not unknown in Europe today; and
they seem to show that democracy can only function
healthily where there is an aristocracy, with a clear law
of succession, to ensure unity and continuity in the state.
At present Eire still lives politically (as she does, even
more, financially) by the light of British tradition and
technique, and we may be thankful for it; but, if she is
not to founder into Communism, she will have to develop
an aristocracy of her own.

I hold no particular brief for the old Protestant gentry
—those Colonels (as I have nicknamed them collectively)
who, in my impatient youth, bored and irritated me beyond all bearing. When I meet any of them today I love
them tenderly, but only because their circumstances are
so very much reduced. They were often good-natured
enough individually; but they committed the unpardon-
able sin, while dwelling among white men, of looking
down upon them as no better than Hottentots. One of

their journals (still in my possession) speaks of the Great Famine as due to "the preposterous redundancy of the population"—that Famine for which the anachronistic system of land-tenure (inherited from Penal times) was so largely responsible. (As an English peer stated in 1843, "in England and Scotland the landlords let farms; in Ireland they only let land".) Up till the passing of the Act of Union, they were in process of turning into an interesting autochthonous species; but ever since that fatal day they accepted the description of themselves as "the Garrison", and tended more and more to be an absentee Garrison—a class, in the most literal and economically vicious sense, of rentiers rather than of landlords. So insulated were they from the life of the people that even W. B. Yeats, as one reads him, sometimes forces one to exclaim "Had he ever spoken to an Irishman?" ("I see a schoolboy, when I think of him"— at a tea-party of the Quality on a wet Sunday, his face and nose pressed against the window.) Though I myself come of their stock, I have also (I am happy to know) some of the blood of the McGraths—a clan always noted, and still notable, for their spirit and physique. One of my Georgian ancestors, as I discovered from some old letters, wedded an Irish lady with the charming name of Sweet Mary Silken Philip (the patronymic following the Christian name according to the Gaelic custom), to repair the wrong he did her in seizing her lands under the Penal Laws. I hope, therefore, that no one will accuse me of pleading for a return to the Bad Old Times in what I have to say.

The drabness which is, to some extent, reasonably complained of in the life of the Irish countryside is due largely, I think, to the now generally-established system of small ownership—that system so often hymned by the English urban littérateur. The houses of the old landlords have been acquired, in very many cases, by religious orders; and whatever their virtues, these do not (unfortunately, in my opinion) make much attempt to brighten or diversify rural life. Those who imagine that peasant proprietorship has infused a new vitality into the Irish countryside should read Mr. Liam O'Flaherty's bitter *Tourist's Guide to Ireland*, or Mr. P. Kavanagh's powerful and pessimistic poem "The Great Hunger":

Nobody will ever know how much tortured poetry the pulled weeds on the ridge wrote
Before they withered in the July sun,
Nobody will ever read the wild, sprawling, scrawling madwoman's signature,
The hysteria and the boredom of the enclosed nun of his thought.
Like the after-birth of a cow stretched on a branch in the wind
Life dried in the veins of these women and men:
The grey and grief and unlove,
The bones in the backs of their hands,
And the chapel pressing its low ceiling over them . . .

Ireland is quickly producing an upper layer of industrialists and Civil Servants; but there is no corresponding rural development, which means incidentally that the interests of the Land—in our agricultural country—go exceedingly ill-represented in parliament and the press. No educated rural class would have tamely tolerated the nonsense of the "Economic War" in the '30s, or the absurd suggestion then heard that you can have greatly increased tillage without manure and imported feeding-stuffs. To waste as little time as possible on this matter (which may seem like a personal foible), the main arguments for reasonably large landowners are the four following. *Firstly*, to employ the landless man and the younger son of the "small man" in his own locality. (The name "peasant", about which Belloc and Chesterton used to grow lyrical, is apt to be resented in Ireland.) It is the small man's unsocial custom to engage the labourer for a few months of the Summer, and then turn him off to hibernate until the harvest comes round again; even then he often gives him his keep only and demands long overtimes, while the big farmer is paying a fairly stiff statute-wage. At other seasons the small man will depend on the unpaid sweated labour of his children —when these are not old enough, or bright enough, to emigrate to the towns. Certainly the relationship of master and man is necessary to bring out the abilities and energies of both; the Arcadian person who is "his own employer" usually tends to have a bad servant—apart from the case of a few creative artists. *Secondly*, to provide, in this manner, a local market for the peasant-farmer—in short, the thing which is so sadly lacking in the Irish country, the village and the life of the village. The complete dependence of the farmer on an urban market—more especially an overseas one—prevents any sane balance between Country and Town, and places Agriculture in the position of the body of Hector (if I may be pardoned a rotund simile) dragged round the chariot-track of the Trade Cycle at the wheels of the Achilleses of Finance. And the small man may well find it worth his while to pay sixpence in rent if he thereby can save a shilling in the middleman's rake-off or the railway's freight. *Thirdly*, to permit of an element of specialism in the rural scene, to balance the all-round amateurishness of the small man (which can be an admirable thing up to a point). There was a day when there were foresters, gardeners, wise old shepherds, carpenters and so forth in Ireland; where, alack, are they now? And for those who care about handicrafts and homebrews, I do not see how these are to come again except by a creative rivalry between villages—each landlord (or more probably his good wife) patronising and vaunting the local product. That at least would seem to me better than going to Quimper or Peru—if you still can get there—in search of "peasant art"; and it has its practical side if Ireland is herself to become—as she well may—a great tourist country. *Fourthly*, to keep things fluid; to permit an efficient labourer to rise into the tenant-class and an inefficient tenant to gravitate to the class where he belongs, that of the labourers. In Ireland land-leases are not now given, except for "eleven months' grazing"; when occupation of land implies ownership, or is apt to imply it, the king of the castle sits tight. Certainly the venerable Irish custom of raising the rent every time the tenant gives his house a new coat of paint is not to be commended. But at present the stigma attaching to "evictions" is such that a farmer, who may spend his time lying in bed, can only with great difficulty be sold up, and land is in consequence not regarded by banks as a "security". This means that Irish farmers, as a class, have not the use of their own savings.

If I were making the laws, I would allow—and encourage—a man to own as much land as he could cover in a morning's walk with his gun and dog, and no more; for on that he could scarcely become a wealthy absentee. Similarly I would allow and encourage him to place as much money as he chose at interest, provided he *spent* his income from it—on his personal estate and dignity; for by that you would not get the famous vicious Capitalist Contradiction. All this would take us too far afield. But I like to think that in Ireland, where the life is simple and the mind has not yet become wholly urbanised, the problems of a new social synthesis may be worked out— as the philosophers found their first metaphysician in the Irishman Berkeley, and as the artists found their first aesthetician in the Irishman Wilde.

However, it may well be that Eire will remain a peasant state. I am quite aware that a proposal to restore "landlordism" would not be greeted—at present, or probably for a long time to come—with any very great popular enthusiasm. Enunciated from an election platform, it might indeed rouse the most dispirited of rural audiences into a state of turbulent animation. One of the best, and fiercest, of Irish popular songs is the maledictory effort which celebrates the death, in the hunting-field, of a certain George Beresford—notorious for his evictions:

O Lord Waterford is dead,
  Says the Shan Van Vocht,
O Lord Waterford is dead,
  Says the Shan Van Vocht,
O Lord Waterford is dead
With the devil at his head,
And 'tis hell will be his bed
  Says the Shan Van Vocht.

They won't put him in the pit,
  Says the Shan Van Vocht,
Where the common sinners sit,
  Says the Shan Van Vocht,
But he'll get a warrum sate
Up beside the special grate
Where his father bakes in state,
  Says the Shan Van Vocht.

So we'll pile a bonfire high,
  Says the Shan Van Vocht,
Till the blazes scorch the sky,
  Says the Shan Van Vocht,
And we'll raise a pillaloo
To be heard in Timbuctoo,
For the devil got his due,
  Says the Shan Van Vocht.

No, the Irish do not hate the English, but they do nourish a traditional dislike—to put it mildly—of landlords. That is partly because many of the Anglo-Irish landlords were really grossly selfish, and partly because the Irish are a proud and somewhat anarchic people. I would not have them different. I can sympathise with the small man's desire to own his family-farm and defend it, like a fort, against "hog, dog or devil". I would only en-

courage him to aim higher, and become himself a gentleman (if that despised word may be allowed) before he is
an owner—and both transitions might be made easier,
for a natural élite, by wise educational and financial
policy. (As an example of less wisely-conceived state-
philanthropy, I remember, when a boy, being constantly
told that Mick or Dick So-and-So had "bought his farm";
on asking how he had managed to do it, I would receive
the invariable, very puzzling, reply, "by non-payment of
rent".) I do not wish to transplant into Ireland the old
English sentiment,

> God bless the Squire and his relations,
> And keep us in our proper stations—

but poor and ignorant owners are apt to be as sterile as
the money-lenders who thrive upon them. There is, of
course, always the danger of the bad landlord; and
though he can be restrained to some extent by legal compulsions, those compulsions are often, I know well
enough, both expensive and ineffectual. Agriculture—
depending as it does on an intimate relationship between
man and man, man and beast, man and soil—is the
most unsuitable of all industries for socialisation; but it
is also the hardest to control under any system of private
property. It is an exceptional inspector who would not be
amenable to the argument of a bottle of wine from the
great man's cellar; and farmers are known to be skilful
at falsifying their returns for Income Tax, when they are
rich enough to be liable for Income Tax. Personally,
I think the risks of having landlords are worth the taking;
for I know of no civilisation whose central stem has not
been the country-house and -estate—I believe that the
best all-round type of human being needs, like a tree, a
certain physical scope and amplitude in which to grow.
But I can understand the farmer who—perhaps with

memories of the rack-renting in his blood—will have none
of such a class. There is, however, a price to be paid for
the Arcadian ideal of "every tenant his own landlord";
it does not make for stability in the state (as the Distri-
butivists fancy)—it makes for anarchy; the line is a thin
one between bolshevism and this sort of agrarian in-
dividualism. The "small man", whose life is one of
grinding toil, can scarcely help having an outlook which
does not extend much further than his hedge; and he will
be peculiarly susceptible to demagogic appeals. By their
insensate hatred and suspicion of the towns, peasants—as
hoarders—are the most inveterate and socially-disastrous
of strikers; they are apt to make bad soldiers but good
mutineers, and they have always shown themselves as
ready—if called upon—to shoot down workmen as to
hang aristocrats. It is much to be feared that, so soon as
British traditions and influences shall have quite faded
away, Eire may turn into a corrupt and disorderly
country—a fate which seems tragically to have befallen
France. Already there are rather ominous signs in the
fragmentation of Irish parties—the appearance of a
medley of groups differing in little but their fairy-tale
Gaelic names ("Children of the People", "Architects of
the Resurrection", etc.). This process is unfortunately-
being accelerated by the system of Proportional Repre-
sentation, so dear to the hearts of some mathematically-
minded idealists—a device originally included in the
Constitution to allay the fears of the Southern Unionists.
If such a political decadence should in fact come about,
all her bishops' pastorals will not preserve Eire from
Communism—or at least from becoming some sort of
dictator-state, with no constitutional safeguards for either
life or property.*

* One agitator has already given me the comforting re-assurance,
in a pamphlet, that I—together with that splendid patron of the

There is, indeed, another and much better possibility; namely, that the Irish peasant should become, like his Dutch or Danish brother, a cooperator and efficient rural industrialist—trained, by some sort of village High-School (very different from that dreary fraud the "Tech"), in the duties of citizenship. In short, that he should lose some of the qualities of a countryman and acquire the virtues of a townsman. That was the hope of what has been irreverently named the "dreamery-cream-ery" school of George Russell and Sir Horace Plunkett; it provided Ireland with a rich fund of good jokes, but otherwise it met with little success. (I remember a story, told to me in contortions of laughter, of a very ambitious cooperative mill which "had cats' and dogs' heads on it" but which never ground even one bag of corn.) However, that slightly prosaic dream might yet be realised—though its first condition, I think, would be the (at present unlikely-seeming) abolition of "Partition", and the opening of the agrarian "South and West" to the ideological penetration of the urban North-East. The result might indeed be a virtual conquest of Ireland by the Ulstermen, and the disappearance of much of what I have called in this book the Irish character. But that would be better, certainly, than the degeneration of Eire into a sort of gunman-ruled South American republic of camarillas and pronunciamientos.

The Irish, it seems to me, have—perhaps more than any other people—the thing called the artistic temperament; which of course is not necessarily the same thing as the artistic faculty. The Irishman is a bohemian and a *j'm'enfoûtiste* in his way of living, somewhat of a play-

arts, Lord Longford—would be "tolerated" if his party should capture power; the implication being, apparently, that a good many other "Anglo-Irishmen" would not be.

actor (or "playboy") alike in action and passion, seeing existence as a *show*—while remaining as far as possible uninvolved. No man is more realistic and cynical conversationally than the artist type of man, but with all his sense of reality he is usually a failure in actual life, because he is not oriented towards a world of facts and duties; and the same is true of the Irishman—he is like the king who never said a foolish thing and never did a wise one. It is a commonplace to speak of the Englishman's sentimental illusions, but he is none the less a huge success in life, because he *is* oriented towards the world of practice. He can indulge himself in sentiment about "the roses round the door" because he has a reassuring sense that there is a policeman round the corner. The Englishman's dreams are his after-dinner relaxation, as the Irishman's jibes are his consolation for an empty stomach. The Englishman's "extroversion" will even make him a success—though not the highest—in art and the things of the spirit, in the rare cases where he has those particular gifts; the Irishman's "introversion" will make him a failure even as an artist or spiritual genius, in the frequent cases where he is naturally so endowed. And allied to the artistic temperament is the humorous temperament, which the Irish admittedly have; and again, though it is less generally recognised, they have not very conspicuously the humorous faculty. The Irish do not *make* jokes, in the manner of the Scots (Shaw— the tireless and unabashed Candid Friend—is to my sense far more Scot than Irishman); they do not recognise a joke to which they are not accustomed; they often do not know that what they are saying is amusing. They simply talk a humorous language. Almost every drollery one hears in Ireland will be found to be (in the Gaelic phrase) "as old as the mist". It is life and love and the flesh—and not any mere trifles—that to the Irishman are ridiculous.

When the English say the Irish have "lost their sense of humour" they are thinking of the "rollicking" Irishman, a character they could like and understand. They liked him for the good reason that he was in fact an Englishman—a colonial variety of the jolly English squire. This type continued in full vigour in Ireland when its exuberance had begun to be curbed in the home-country by the rising middleclass and the nonconformist conscience. It persisted, with all the greater obstreperousness, owing to the fact that after the Union and Catholic Emancipation the gentry felt no further responsibility for the country, and had a general sense of "Après nous le déluge". It is no wonder that the English found in Ireland the land of their dreams! A friend of mine, now dead, was a somewhat extreme example of this rake-helly race. He lived—or camped—in a huge mansion, which had been so thoroughly combed by bailiffs that it was destitute of even the meanest conveniences. Many rooms were windowless, and, as the country-people said, "The curlews flew in and out of them". His salons, his library, his cellar, his racing-stables—all these were, when I knew him, already legend; though a gorgeous legend. There remained little except a pair of heavy silver candlesticks, which at his parties—or rather orgies—sometimes served as missiles, testifying to his strength of arm. On these occasions one sat on packing-cases, and slept where—and when—one dropped. His delight was to challenge the more suicidally-minded among his guests to jump through a certain high window into an area, a feat which one of his ancestors—in full flight from the duns—was said to have accomplished unscathed. On one occasion the wager was accepted, and the rash "taker" had to be forcibly restrained by the soberer members of the company. For a more-than-Charlotte Brontë touch of horror, my friend was known to have several children, all of them out of their wits, but existing in some remote part of his forlorn residence. His pranks were endless, and there were many which I could not recount in print in a country which has a censorship; a typical one was to ride a kicking cob into a crowded dance-hall. However, peace to him! He died, in a gallant and daring exploit, in the Second World War; and the place of his revels was re-garnished and sanctified, passing into the careful hands of a community of nuns. There is nothing particularly Irish about such a character—a type of man rather over-romanticised by W. B. Yeats and Dr. Oliver Gogarty; it is simply 18th Century, without the greater 18th-Century qualities. The Georgians, at least in the finer second half of the century, were more than mere roisterers; they were—many of them—builders, landscape-gardeners, fine speakers in public and writers in privacy. The evidence is there in their mansions— often built without the employment of a professional architect, in the lay-out of their estates, in the diaries of such men as Barrington. They may have been British colonists—though they would have resented the term— but they were not provincials. They were something more than the "Garrison" type from which they origi- nated—and to which, unfortunately, they reverted.

That late-18th Century world was, I repeat, not Irish —or not yet fully so; but I think it is a pity it guttered out as it did. Ireland might have evolved into a prosperous, conservative and agricultural community to balance the development of democratic industrial England—with mutual benefit; the barren and dismal solution of "buying out the landlords" might never have been the necessity that in fact it became. It is even possible that the gentry would have tended to turn Catholic, by mar- riage with the older stock, and that Irish Catholicism would not have become what Provost Mahaffy called it—

"essentially the religion of the lower orders". The Irish people have the artist-temperament, which is near to the aristocrat's temperament; they have not, and I doubt if they ever will have, the particular virtues and vices of a bourgeoisie. The only really bourgeois Irishman is the Ulsterman of the North-East counties, and he (generally speaking) is an unpleasing hybrid; he has the hardness of the Lowland Scot without his urbanity. It may be said that every race receives its stamp and colour from its superior caste. The Irish, in modern times, have had no native upper caste except the priesthood, with the consequence that the typical Irishman is a little like a priest; since there are no such things in a Christian land as priestesses, the Irishwoman has remained a little more natural, a little closer to the earth. But if civilisation is to continue, which seems at the moment of writing doubtful, Ireland—it is to be hoped—will have her upper caste, and the national character will accordingly become richer and more positive. I do not venture to predict what that more developed Irish character will be like; but I believe I can see its ground-plan traced in the thought of two 18th-Century Anglo-Irishmen—Jonathan Swift and George Berkeley. Though children of the alien race and religion, they exhibited, and stated in a challenging form, what seem to me the two unchanging halves of the Irish mind: a fear and distrust of the Natural Man—especially the Mass-Man—and a disbelief in this solid-seeming law-driven material world. They are also, I think, the two qualities of which humanity in this century has most need. The Irishman is claustrophobic —he dislikes living in large urban aggregations; when he does so—in the Irish quarters of British and American cities—it is for self-protection against an alien, godless, environment. At the same time the world of today, as I need hardly point out, is altogether bedevilled with mass-values and quantitative standards; it has set up an ideal more vulgar than any idol of the past—and one certainly no less bloodthirsty—the ideal represented by such concepts as the Ordinary Man, the Average Man, the Man in the Street. Even the Platonist Dr. Joad has to make himself common in style and manner before he can be listened to; even the highly-cultivated German nation accepted Hitler *because* he was ugly, mean and insignificant, as the servant-girl falls for the commercial traveller. In such a world Swift, under his great epitaph in St. Patrick's, still seems to give superb expression to our refusal to "join in the racket". And the significance for us of Berkeley is similar. The Irishman is always at odds with Matter—with this lower and contingent Creation. He has a long-standing reputation as a fine craftsman, a cool organiser, a brilliant social charmer; but he is also commonly known as just the opposite of all these—as the veriest sloven and marplot. What is more remarkable is that the virtuosity and the ineptitude are often found in the same man. You can never be sure of him—he is apt to spoil everything by some sudden freak of flippancy, of impatience, or of conceit. With him it is not even one step from the sublime to the ridiculous; it is as if some Bad Fairy were always twitching at his sleeve. The positive side of this is that the Irishman's eye can create and transform, where his hand is apt to mar and destroy. He knows in his heart that man's problem is not to *set* things right but to *see* them rightly; "the old people who believed in pishogues (superstitions) were happier than we" he says—I have heard the surprising statement made repeatedly in Ireland. This is also an unpopular school of thought in the world today; it is supposed that Matter is patient of being controlled, planned, rationalised—to almost any extent. The words of H. G. Wells are echoed, in various ways, by almost every living thinker, "I see no limit to it at all." The professors of the Academy of Lagado now promise us an *Ersatz* world— perhaps in time an *Ersatz* man. Formerly, the moderns tell us, man was a dreamer; now, he has laid hold on Matter and will make it serve him. By concentrating upon its two modes of Mass and Movement, and neglecting the rest, he has—he believes—found the perfect formula for everything. But a voice from the quiet 18th Century bishopric of Cloyne still repeats its classic, ringing, challenge: "We Irishmen think otherwise."

The Irishman, as I see him, is something of a realist and something of a mystic. In his literature he wavers continually between fantasy and farcicality; his most successful *genre*—from the Cuchulainn epic to *Ulysses*—is a sort of surrealistic extravaganza which has no precise parallel elsewhere. He is instinctively bored by the Good, sceptical of the True, and distrustful of the Beautiful. Like Swift, he feels vividly that Matter is dirt and that Man is an unclean, irreclaimable, animal; he has never got far enough from the farm to have the questionable illusion of "immaculate cleanliness"—an illusion so near-related to the modern townsman's dream of perfectibility. On the other hand, like Berkeley, he knows that this material world is a trick, unwearyingly repeated, of that very old-Gaelic magician the light, and that truth must be both nearer and farther from us than the sun. Man as knowing Subject is a God—as the object who is known he is the Yahoo; these truths, expressed in the older language of his faith, he holds to be self-evident. They are, of course, extreme and inhuman truths, inappropriate perhaps—if held in this intensity—for ordinary striving men; in combination they produce the Irishman's temperament of an almost priest-like mildness, varying with explosions of startling, apparently causeless, fury. In the normal man of other nations they are reconciled and

moderated by sexual love, in which the "object" becomes
a little less objectionable, the "subject" a little less sub-
jective and detached. This solution the Irish refuse—or
would like to refuse; not, I think, so much from moral
prejudice as from a taste for taking ideas in almost
chemical purity—like a taste for mathematics, or a taste
for whisky. They refuse the Great Compromise, the
Supreme Derogation, of passion. The Irishman is apt
to be a late reveller, but he is so only because he prefers
the starlit deserted alleys to the hot market-place in
which other men work and play. And I cannot end this
study better than by quoting the great line of the 17th-
Century Gaelic poet, David O'Bruadar—a line so im-
pregnated with every Irish quality that it fills me with a
deep sense of the futility of my laborious prose:—

> 'Tis time at length for me to foot it homewards,
> For the poets of the world lie sleeping.*

---

* Is mithid damhsa bann do bhaile
  Ó táid éigse an ché in a gcadladh.

APPENDIX

The following talk upon "the Contemporary Thought of Ireland" *was given by the writer in* 1947 *on the B.B.C. Third Programme and from Radio Eireann. It was also printed in* "The Listener", "The Dublin Magazine" *and in* "The Irish Association Bulletin".

It must be confessed that the subject on which I have to address you is a singularly unpromising one. Indeed I may say that the thought of having to speak on the Thought of Ireland has been weighing unpleasantly on my mind. In our country, schools of philosophy do not exactly teem; one may doubt whether the idealist aesthetic of Benedetto Croce or the existentialism of Jean-Paul Sartre has aroused a flicker of interest among our intellectuals, from poets to professors. And this is to name only the two most discussed doctrines which have appeared in Europe since 1914.

Even if philosophers like Croce or Sartre were to arise in our midst, it is probable that they would remain as unheard of as would, say, a real creative writer in Irish, for philosophy like Irish is a language—a language taught and venerated in schools, but, like Irish, usually regarded as totally useless and without the least relation to real life. The one personality we have to show in this century who approached the stature of a leader of thought was the interesting and versatile George Russell; but Russell's mind hovered between Celticism and Orientalism, between Tara and Tibet, and somehow skipped Europe—where the world's thinking, hardened in the fires of action, has been chiefly carried on. Whatever may be the final assessment of A. E.'s life and work—and I am one of those who think he was over-rated during his life as he is perhaps over-neglected today—it must be said of him that his personality gave a serious and enquiring bent to all the minds it touched, and that he made Dublin during his lifetime what it has never quite been since, an intellectual capital. Our two best poets—I refer to Mr. Austin Clarke and Mr. Seumas O'Sullivan—still carry about them some of the glory of that time, before civil war came to extinguish the Candle of Vision. In a world which seems to be groping its way back to what A. E. called the Oversoul, what Aldous Huxley calls the Divine Ground, and what we may non-committally call the Values of the Contemplative Life, it is likely that George Russell will be remembered as a forerunner—a true artist philosopher, though perhaps too little of a philosopher or an artist. Such undoubtedly greater men as W. B. Yeats and George Moore, who towards the end of their lives seemed to be turning their attention to philosophy and religion, never hesitated to admit their debt to Russell. But in them one is made aware, for good and ill, as in A. E. one is not, of the escapist side of the Irish genius—even though it is an ironic escapism; an interest in ideas as a refuge from the facts rather than an interpretation of them, an attraction to the world of thought as a "Land of Youth" for pagan myth-heroes born out of time.

This may be seen in Yeats' discovery, and misconception, of Bishop Berkeley. For Yeats saw in the Berkeleian idealism an affirmation of the anarchy of imagination, a Magna Carta for the poet's licence, a resolution of the world into a dream. But this would have horrified the devout Berkeley, who wished to turn back the anarchy and licence of atheistic philosophers by making them question their own assumptions. Berkeley was a great Irishman, who fought the sceptics of his time as Socrates

fought the sophists of his, trying to establish firm foundations for knowledge; but there is a tendency among some
of the Anglo-Irish to make him a *ne plus ultra* in philosophy, whereas his mind was wholly 18th Century and
conservative. His paradox that "Matter does not exist"
is the first word and not the last word of metaphysics; as
Messrs. Hone and Rossi have shown in their excellent
"Life", he was in reality a sturdy defender of common
sense in the age of common sense. He had no suspicion
of the monstrous forms which philosophic idealism would
assume in the next two centuries; when he said "To be
is to be perceived" he did not foresee that the world
would become something very like a cracked looking-
glass for the Yahoo, or that his idealistic tar-water would
be strained until nothing remained of it but pitch.

The school of Roman Catholic neo-Thomism is in
large measure a reaction against this cracked-looking-
glass philosophy of idealism—this dream of the mind
closed in upon itself—for materialism in the 19th-
Century sense may be said to be defunct in the present
age, if we overlook America. Neo-Thomism has not yet
got its Irish Maritain, and can hardly yet be said to be the
vital force one would expect it to be in Ireland; though it
has given a direction to one or two of our better poets,
like Mr. Robert Farren and Mr. Thomas McGreevy.
But in the main our writers seem to think they can preserve a virginal neutrality in this world of warring ideas,
an "art for art's sake" without even the courage of that
rather ascetic doctrine. If they show the intellectual pug-
nacity upon which we used to pride ourselves, it is only to
attack censorship or to praise Marxist Communism. I
am not going to discuss here whether these attitudes are
right or wrong; I would only point out that they are in-
consistent with each other. One feels the lack of a syn-
thesising philosophy of life, one misses a realisation of the

anguish of the modern consciousness—such as is shown, for instance, by the French existentialists, who bravely seek to snatch a reason for living out of despair itself.

A young Frenchman said to me recently "We have no time to be amused". We in Ireland, it would seem, have all the time there is to be amused; but the world no longer laughs with us, and we are somewhat in the position of the Court Jester out of court. I say this—and I immediately relent towards my fellow-countrymen; for our mental frivolity preserves us, after all, from what is the curse of most philosophy, especially in the English tongue—a portentous and bombinating seriousness. I am of the opinion that there are stray aphorisms scattered through Wilde's *Intentions* and *The Soul of Man under Socialism* which are worth most of the books of philosophy written in England during the 19th Century. Even in the present paper famine, ponderous tomes issue from the presses with such titles as *Emergent Evolution* or *Religion in the Making*—to quote the linguistically barbarous heading of a work by a famous contemporary philosopher. I think we may be grateful to be saved from the present craze of evolutionary humanism in thought, as in the Victorian Age we were saved from the neo-Gothic fashion in architecture—less perhaps by our taste than by our isolation. I believe that the Irish mind is imbued with a deep innate disillusionment and disbelief in life, that was here even before Christianity came to our shores and found such a quick response in our people. Though we are fond of dreams and enchantments, we play with them, and are not generally their slaves; we desire them only because we are already disenchanted with the reality. It is this which distinguishes us above all from that other great legend-loving race, the Germans—in whose sagas the Unknown is always represented by a witch or nixie, alluring, irresistible and dangerous.

The novel *Murphy*, by an expatriate Dubliner, Samuel Beckett, expresses this contradiction in a bitterly farcical form; its hero determines to become an attendant in a lunatic-asylum. He prefers the mad to the sane *because* they are mad—not because he loves madness, but because he hates the sensibly-ordered world more. As he says, he thinks of the patients "not as banished from a system of benefits but as escaped from a colossal fiasco". Unlike most modern novels which may be called pathological, in *Murphy* the hero's tone remains cool, reasoned and sane; even when he is most mad, the Irishman is a little of a conscious ironist and play-actor. A similar philosophy of life is expressed in Synge's beautiful play *The Well of the Saints*, in which two old people, cured of blindness, deliberately ask to be restored to the Kingdom of the Blind, because (so to speak) in that kingdom every man is a king and every woman a queen. The dream is desired *because* it is a dream—with a clear-eyed choice. This tendency of ours can seem exceedingly irritating and ostrich-like today—though, as Murphy in one place remarks, who knows what the ostrich sees in the sand? But I think nevertheless that it holds a promise for to-morrow. For whether or no the world as a whole returns to orthodox religion, it will certainly return—if it is to survive—to more sober estimates of human nature and possibilities than have been fashionable in the age which has followed the French Revolution, the age of that delirious "Progress" which has largely been the Progress of the Rake, and of which we are already experiencing the hang-over.

More than that, if civilisation is to survive it must rediscover and allow for that disabused detachment of the individual, that obstinate refusal to be involved, which I regard as a peculiarly Irish characteristic—a sense of the word "individuality" which was largely missed during

the era of political liberalism. In the more strictly philosophical field, I believe that Ireland may yet have a word
to say in the 20th Century, as she had through John
Scotus in the 9th Century and through Bishop Berkeley
in the 18th—in both cases introducing a new era of
thought by a daring feat of simplification. For philosophy has now to give us back, by an act of transcendental
imagination, the shape and design of the external world—
the world of which, through an era of analysis, she has
progressively robbed and impoverished our souls; and
this task demands a combination of realism and religious
feeling nowhere else but here to be found, I think, among
modern men. The new synthesis that I look forward to
will proceed, if I am right, above all from artists; for art,
as Mr. Cecil Salkeld once defined it in conversation with
me, is "the maximum of association with the minimum
of form"—a definition which brilliantly combines modern
physical and ancient metaphysical formulae for the cos-
mos. But in making this prophecy, I cheerfully admit, I
am guided by faith—some will say by wishful thinking—
rather than by reason; for Ireland at present might as
well be the Gobi Desert for any tangible evidence that
out of her will come a school of philosophy. But when
one reflects on the impact made upon the imagination of
the world by Shaw, W. B. Yeats and Joyce, it is hard to
believe that Ireland has become a No-Man's-Land of the
mind, or that she has grown provincial at the moment
when she is, for the first time after centuries, a nation.

When intelligent visitors to our country are asked about
their impressions of us, they usually pay us many kind and
—we will hope—deserved compliments, but they generally end by commenting on our truly staggering indifference to events in the outer world. This shows, I
think, the dangerous side of that detached spirit of which
I have already emphasised the positive and hopeful side.

I do not want to raise here the question of what a country-man called our "neuterality"; in that matter we took a position I think both legitimate and dignified. But I do consider it a disgrace that freedom-loving Irishmen of intelligence could be heard to defend, as I have heard them defend, the behaviour of the German equivalent of the Black-and-Tans to the brave Catholic Poles. I hasten to leave this controversial subject; but the fact remains that a European consciousness can hardly be said to exist in Ireland. Far too many Irish people talk as if we were the pure, the uncontaminated, a race apart, shining like a good deed in a naughty world. A tight-lipped and censorious book on Voltaire appeared last year, with the *imprimatur* of the President of Cork University; in it many of the Sage of Ferney's best quips were held up to indignant opprobrium. This is the sort of thing that gives us that reputation for a rancid prudery formerly enjoyed chiefly by Anglo-Saxons. Sometimes one really wonders why we do not erect a statue to Oliver Cromwell, since the Puritan has become our Patron Saint.

But it would be unfair to suggest, as is sometimes suggested, that there is no constructive social and economic thought going on in Ireland; for there are some interesting trends to be noticed among both the principal religious groups—trends of which the class specifically called, or self-called, intellectuals seems to be very little aware. I may mention the interesting and provocative book on *Money* by the afore-mentioned President of Cork University, the stimulating pamphlets of the "Towards a New Ireland" series, the books of Mr. Arnold Marsh, and especially that brilliant and entertaining modernisation of Berkeleian economics—the anonymous pamphlet called *The New Querist*. With the particular economic thought developed in these works—that known in England as "The New Economics", and expounded every week by a group of gifted writers in *The New English Weekly*—I cannot deal here; nor indeed would I be competent to deal with it anywhere. But those who equally dislike complete collectivism and *laissez faire* capitalism would do better to search for the humanly-tolerable pattern of society than spend their time in bewailing the hold of religion on the popular mind. Fifty years ago, many educated people regarded religion as an obscurantist force. Today the position is changed, and the religious bodies are almost the only groups over much of the world which still stand for elementary liberties and sanities. To give one small and telling example: torture, for accidents of birth or opinion, used to be associated with the name of the Spanish Inquisition. The Spanish Inquisition looks almost like a tea-party today. From this fact people will draw varying conclusions. I am a member of no church, and my own conclusions would perhaps not be orthodox. But that it *is* a fact there can be no reasonable dispute.

I would like to add a few remarks on Contemporary Thought in the Irish language; but for the unfortunate circumstance that there is no thought whatever being produced in Irish—unless one may give that title to some of the more inspired witticisms of Myles na gCopaleen. (I heard today that a young plumber was writing a poem in Irish on existentialism. If it is true, I apologise to him.) Irish is, nevertheless, no matter how often we hear assertions to the contrary, a medium very well adapted to the finer distinctions of the mind. My friend the poet and economist Francis Macnamara, who died last year, was struck by the fact that Gaelic has two words for the concept "good"—the one always placed before, and the other after, its noun—and similarly with the concept "bad". He saw in this an attempt to distinguish between

the individual quality that comes from within, and the
social character which is imposed from without. Most of
what I have tried to say here might perhaps be expressed
simply by saying that we in Ireland still prefer the *deagh-
dhuine* to the *duine maith*. To translate, very inadequately
—we care more for the Man than for the mere good
citizen. That, maybe, is our greatest hope.

8 111211M 9 9

W121, 19018

17 9 9

12N 5 4